EDUMATCH SNAPSHOT IN EDUCATION 2019

MARVIA DAVIDSON   JAMIE P. SPIKERMAN, M.ED.
CLARA ALANIZ   KATE WEBER   KIMBER JOHNSTON
MELISSA-ANN PERO   WINIFRED A. WINSTON
JESSICA REED, ED.S.   AUBREY JONES
ADRIENNE SCHLAKE   DR. JASON TRUMBLE
CHARLES WEBER   KATHLEEN H. FULLER, M.S.ED.
JASON TRINH   MELODY MCALLISTER
MARIO CHRISTINER   RACHELLE DENE POTH
DAVID LOCKETT   DR. SAM FECICH   BRIAN KULAK
DR. DEBORAH KERBY   DR. MARQUITA BLADES
DYANN WILSON   DR. RAYE WOOD   JASON B. ALLEN

JEFFREY BRADBURY   ANDREA TRUDEAU   AMY STORER
ERIN B. KIGER   KRISTEN KOPPERS, M.ED., NBCT

Edited by
SARAH-JANE THOMAS, PHD

Copyright © 2019

Published by EduMatch®
PO Box 150324, Alexandria, VA 22315
www.edumatchpublishing.com

All rights reserved. No portion of this book may be reproduced in any form without permission from the publisher, except as permitted by U.S. copyright law. For permissions contact sarah@edumatch.org.

ISBN: 978-1-970133-51-6

DEDICATION

This book is dedicated to the EduMatch® family of educators. Thank you to those of you who have been so willing to share, as we continue to learn and grow together.

ACKNOWLEDGMENTS

Thank you to the following chapter editors, who helped to make this book possible:

Irene Bal (Ch. 1)
Marvia Davidson (Ch. 18)
Heather Gauck (Ch. 28)
Salandra Grice (Ch. 13)
Teresa Gross (Ch. 3)
Laurie Guyon (Ch. 26)
Kristin Harrington (Ch. 5)
Kristen Koppers (Ch. 9)
Dr. Jacie Maslyk (Ch. 20)
Melody McAllister (Ch. 12)
Rachelle Dene Poth (Ch. 25)
Elissa Waingort (Ch. 14)
Dr. Melissa Dandy Walker (Ch. 19)
Jeannie Timken (Ch. 13)

CONTENTS

Part One
PART ONE: TEACHING PRACTICES

1. You Cannot Be Afraid to Teach	3
2. A Secondary Experience	11
3. The Impact of Positive Relationships	19
4. Mindful, Not Mind Full	27
5. "That might work with some students…"	41
6. Going Gradeless	47
7. Educators, Get Comfortable with the Uncomfortable: Dyslexia	51
8. Collaborative Co-Teaching in the Classroom	61
9. The Beauty of Collaboration	67
10. Leveling Up With Digital Badges	73
11. Gaming Business Education - Let's Play!	85

Part Two
PART TWO: IDENTITY

12. Adding to the Single Story	99
13. Race Matters for this White Teacher	105

Part Three
PART THREE: PREPARING FOR THE FUTURE

14. How to Prepare Students for their Future?	117
15. Preparing for the Future	129
16. Learning with IoT	141
17. Preparing Student Teachers with a sprinkle of EduMagic	145

Part Four
PART FOUR: TAKING CARE OF OURSELVES (AND EACH OTHER)

18. #SEL4ADULTS	163
19. Staying positive in the K-12 classroom	171
20. Re-Inventing Yourself After Experiencing Teacher Burnout	177

21. #SelfCare is Not Just a Hashtag	183
22. Teacher Self-Care: Why it is Necessary	189

Part Five
PART FIVE: ALL HANDS ON DECK

23. Black Parents Must Be Engaged in School Turnaround Work	201
24. Should You Hire A Tech Coach ... Or A Tech Conductor?	207
25. School Librarians: The Unsung Heroes in Education	217
26. Teachers Deserve it Too	223

Part Six
PART SIX: TELLING OUR STORIES

27. Undrcaff3inatED: A Podcast Story	231
28. First Impressions Will Make a Difference	237
Notes	245
Other EduMatch Titles	247

PART ONE: TEACHING PRACTICES

YOU CANNOT BE AFRAID TO TEACH

Marvia Davidson

Teaching is hard but worth it work; so let's show up and keep showing up.

There's nothing like the excitement of the first days of school and a new teaching assignment. I still remember my first year teaching and the hope and idealism I held when I walked into my very own classroom. I was nervously excited. Several months after graduating from college, I was stepping into a southside, high school English classroom with students who were not too far in age from me.

Everyday took courage to show up and work with the young men and women who came from diverse backgrounds. There were many days I questioned my ability, my skills, and my sanity. Though I faced doubt, apprehension, and many different challenges in my years of teaching, one thought has remained constant: I cannot and should NOT be afraid to teach!

BE UNAFRAID

You cannot be afraid to teach.

Nope. Not at all. Not one iota. No fear.

To teach is to engage in fierce work. It is the work of transformation. It is the work of nurturing and growing students into who they're meant to be.

Teaching and leading in schools is change agent work. We're advocates, supporters, learners, instructors, bridge builders, and sometimes disruptors of the status quo. It is a meticulous and sometimes tedious process because we're building and reaffirming foundations so students have solid ground to navigate this 21st century world. The work can be tireless.

Tenacity and critical questioning are a gift when we're facing change. One thing I've learned to embrace this year is to quickly recognize when change is happening and to identify my role in it. I have to ask myself what the root issue is and how I work through it. Asking questions through a change can also help us get to the root of our schools' challenges so we can best serve our students. It is a work in which there is no room for fear. It is something I remind myself in the moments where shift in thinking and change of process are happening. Of course, these things seem to be constantly happening in the field of education.

TEACHING WITHOUT FEAR

If to teach is to forever touch a life, then to teach without fear is to always be a learner. It is to be unafraid of undoing our own misconceptions and misguided thinking. It is means we confront oppression, aggression, suppression, and all those things that keep students and ourselves from engaging and living with purpose, authenticity, and intention. It is to work from a place of security and not fear when change is underfoot.

Change happens. It's always going to happen. We can see the shifts in our educational, political, and social systems. Though some of the shifting may seem disruptive, we cannot be afraid to work through the change as it is happening. We cannot be afraid to stand firm in our beliefs and ideas. We cannot be afraid to ask critical questions along the way. When I find myself in the middle of a shift, I choose to remember that I cannot be afraid to move through the change nor question the change as it is occurring.

Any shift or change I want to see must first begin in me, and I cannot be afraid to embrace it. I am the shift. I am the change. I am one part of this moving wheel, and so are each of you. Again, these words ring in my ears, "you cannot be afraid to teach!"

THE SHOW-UP MOMENT

The question now becomes: what do we do now? This is the show-up moment. Educators near and far, it's time to show up. Show up as your WHOLE self: imperfect, jaded, growing, learning, making mistakes, relearning, unlearning, being okay with temporary discomfort, and unabashedly embracing all of what it means to be a true lifelong learning educator. Show up and engage! Do not allow fear to keep you from engaging in this work. Be a part of the equation. Spark the conversation. Challenge the assumption that your voice doesn't matter. Advocate for your students so they have what they need to get to where they want to be. Ask the difficult questions. Show up, and sit at the table to represent the voices of the students who keep showing up in your room. Show up!

THIS my educator friends, is how we fight the fear we may face when change comes. We show up. We raise our voices to be heard. We refuse to allow fear to derail our purpose and the value of the work we do. We refuse to subjugate ourselves to the opinion of the masses who have no "skin in the game." We refuse to be silent. We will raise our words. We will confront our own foolishness, ignorance, and bias. We cannot be afraid.

So much of what we "teach" is revealed in how we "are" and not only what we "do." Our students and communities are depending on us to do what is good and right and to pose the critical questions about the decisions being made. Our children are watching how we model the ideals we champion. They are watching what we do more than listening to what we say. They are watching how we show up, so let's show up!

The work we do is sacred, challenging, beautiful, arduous, and precious. It matters. You matter. You are a change maker; so don't you dare give up now. You cannot be afraid to teach. Repeat after me: "I cannot be afraid to teach!"

Marvia Davidson

ABOUT THE AUTHOR

Marvia was a high school English teacher for over a decade in public, private, and charter schools in Texas before becoming a campus administrator. She is currently serving as a school improvement coordinator. She has worked with students and teachers from diverse backgrounds, and loves helping students realize their potential. As a lifelong learner, Marvia loves growing her PLN, CoffeeEdu meet-ups, and collaborating with educators on how to do what's best for students and teachers to bring positive change. She's not only an educator but an avid mixed media artist who enjoys lettering, painting, and baking. She is committed to learner and teacher development. Connect with Marvia at @marviadavidson on Twitter, Instagram, LinkedIn, and Voxer. You can also find her writing, making, and creating on her site at marviadavidson.com.

A SECONDARY EXPERIENCE
Jamie P. Spikerman, M.Ed.

After a decade of dealing out "elementary hope", a secondary experience is just what I needed.

If we take a moment to be honest with each other, we would admit we all just want to be accepted for who we are, feel safe, and fun sometimes. We are very good at fostering those needs in the elementary setting, and one look at social media shows we never cease in reminding adults of their "inner child" and encouraging them to celebrate self-care. But, what about the messy middle? Being a teenager is a turbulent stage of life. One week into my first year as a school counselor, it was obvious that my brand of what a colleague would later label as "elementary hope" was just what high school students were craving.

Let me back up, though, because my background is important. I was an elementary classroom teacher for over a decade. I focused on making connection the center of my classroom. When the "class family" movement started to gain popularity, I was all about it. Now, I am not saying that was something unique I did—most teachers were about it. If I ran into a teacher who flat out refuted and ignored the idea of taking the time to establish a classroom home and make connections, it was rare. (But, if you've been in education long enough, you know toxic teachers unfortunately still exist.) The point being, the elementary setting, in general, is hopeful and colorful and nurturing. We focus on soft skills like good citizenship, respecting boundaries, having fun and spreading joy. If you walk into the right K-5 classroom on any given day, you're going to walk out feeling joy or exhaustion—most of the time both. Because raising good people is hard work, or as I love to say, heart work.

I took on a few leadership roles and ran some professional development here and there, but whenever I was asked if I had plans to get my M.Ed., I would always say, "Nope! I love it in the classroom!" Thank goodness I never said "Never!" because—well, you should never say never!

I clearly remember the day I went home and told my husband I wanted to start working toward my M.Ed. That morning, I had walked into an ARD meeting prepared to advocate for one of my students because I had taken enough time to peel back some layers of "stuff" to discover he was great at math. But, his IEP goals were antiquated. I prepared for this ARD like I had never before. I typed up notes, I photocopied proof of his progress. I was ready (and very excited) to showcase his growth in my third-grade math and science classroom. I don't remember the specific moment my enthusiasm and advocacy started to go south. But, I do remember the moment that changed the entire trajectory of my career. We were working on setting his IEP goals, and I had begun to, again, state my case that this young boy no longer needed a math goal that basically sentenced him to practicing addition facts repeatedly. It was that point in an ARD meeting when a teacher can feel as though everyone is so used to going through the motions that they're missing the point of the meeting altogether—to review, advocate, and encourage a student toward further success. The worst feeling is when a teacher feels she isn't being heard. So, I begin again, and I am cut off by my administrator with words that I can hear to this day. She said, "We get it. You care."

Let that sink in for a minute.

She was annoyed that I was fervently advocating, and that I CARED. She said that out loud. To me. In front of a committee of peers. Somewhere after that, I vaguely remember the special education teacher (who came to my room to work with this student) spoke up and started showing us a "wonderful strategy" for the student to continue working on math facts to 20. Sure, wonderful—if the student did not already know them. Guess what, that math goal didn't change. Shocker, I know. I remember leaving in tears and trying to get out quickly before any (more) committee members noticed the anxious ball of heartache and fury shaking as she walked out of the room.

Two quick and exhausting years later, I was standing in Reed Arena at Texas A&M University, waiting for my moment to walk across that stage and receive my M. Ed. in Educational Psychology: Creativity and Cognition. Yes, I will put that whole title right there. Because I am damn proud of myself. I was a wife, a mom of two active kids and one adult forever daughter, and I taught full-time. Oh, and I didn't just teach any grade. I taught Kindergarten. Yes, on purpose. I asked to move from third to Kinder because I knew I wouldn't have papers to grade at night and I could focus on grad school. There were days where I would wrangle, redirect and love on my five-year-olds for eight hours. Then come home, briefly parent and see my own kids (I have an amazing hubby!), and stay up all night writing a research paper, just to shower, grab some coffee, and head back to the tiny army awaiting me at school that morning. So, I think if you survive something that (quite literally) nearly kills you, you have a free pass to talk about it incessantly for the rest of your life. For me, that was grad school (and its partner in crime, student loan debt).

As the end of the 2017-18 school year approached, I was on FIRE. I was reaching out to anyone and everyone within the district where I worked, seeking out a new position to go with my shiny new title. This district was my home. The one I trust with my own children's education. I was eager but, looking back, I was also incredibly naive. I thought, "They love me. I lead PD sessions, I am part of the super's leadership academy, I am a tech mentor, I have a great rapport with families. It was a no-brainer. If there is a school counseling spot, I was a shoo-in for it."

I was also wrong.

In the end, I ended up down the road in a district I knew nothing about but decided to interview because it was a reasonable drive from home. This new district was able to offer me the one thing the district I consider "home" could not—a chance.

That chance, which I am now so thankful for, circles me back to what I now call my 'secondary experience.' I was not only starting what felt like, at the time, a secondary choice. But, I was also moving from elementary school (kindergarten to be exact)—to the unfamiliar world of secondary education.

So, here I am in high school. I find this second time around way more fun, might I add, because being a teenager is HARD. And trying to figure out who you are and what you stand for is no easy task. High school can make a teenager think they should know these answers or pretend until they do. It's messy. It's dramatic. It's uncertain. In my first week with the students I was replaying all those typical high school experiences—but with a new, outside lens. I wanted to get to know all the kids, all 800 of them! I did the only things I've ever known to do with kindergarteners: bribe them. What, were you expecting a complicated lesson plan and detailed research? I taught elementary and I know kids like bribes. I also have teens and I know they are just as intrigued by "what's in it for me?" as a five-year-old with the offer of candy to celebrate a "good day." That's the only research I need.

So, I set a glass jar full of candy in the sight line of any student passing by my office. I filled a bookshelf with things that had spent a lifetime in my elementary classroom—fidget spinners, playing cards, squishies and stress balls, a slinky, coloring books, and even a mini set of Jenga blocks. The most loved chair from my classroom that students lovingly named "the green monster" came up as well. Then, I waited. It didn't take long. On the second day of school, I met Peter, an energetic and quick witted sophomore who came bounding in to give me a hug and meet me—and to walk out with a piece of candy from that jar. I think he has come by my office every day since. And, he isn't the only one. I have a group that hangs before the morning bell. I have the cutest little couple that stops by together, unless of course, they are having a spat—then they visit separately. I have one girl who I am pretty sure I would adopt if she didn't already have a loving home. And, all the new freshmen! Oh my gosh, you know, there are some times when my freshmen remind me of all my kindergarten babies who I miss so much.

I got some curious looks from peers and admin in the beginning. Once, I was even told by a colleague I have come to absolutely appreciate that I had "elementary hope." I was consoling a teenager that was in such distress she was a puddle of tears and snot. I didn't even think twice before grabbing a Kleenex and wiping her face clean. Remember, I had spent time in Kindergarten, face-wiping is an unconscious reflex for me. That was the first time I heard this colleague coin the term "elementary hope," and I hope to never ever hear the last time.

I am not sure they knew what to do with a high school counselor whose first mission was to paint her office a bright, cheerful color and fill it with toys and candy. Then she goes and designates one of her office walls to be a place just for students to sign their names. But, I am now entering my second year and my office is still that place—a safe place. Not just for the students I am 'assigned' on a team of counselors. Any student that I took the extra two minutes to connect with, or support, or comfort, or to just hear. That's the biggest reason I notice kids keep coming back: I gave them space to be present and I listen without judgment.

Teens can be just as exhausting as kindergarteners, so I was well prepared for that need. They can also be just as playful and need just as much love, support, and grace. If not more. In just over a year, I have experienced every celebration, fear, and heartache that you can imagine may bring a teenager to their school counselor. I also hear things every day that remind me I am EXACTLY where I am supposed to be. Things like, "Why are you so nice?", "How do you already know my name?", "You know how to spell my name!? No one does!", "Can I come by __ period just to talk something out with you?" and my favorite, "I love you, Mrs. Spikerman."

You know who else said that all the time? My elementary kiddos. So, you see, sometimes having a wealth of experience in dealing out "elementary hope" is just what a high school teenager needs. And, I am happy to be their hope dealer.

∼

Jamie P. Spikerman, M.Ed.

ABOUT THE AUTHOR

Jamie Spikerman is a veteran teacher who transitioned to the high school setting as a counselor in 2018 after over a decade in the elementary classroom setting. Her philosophy on education is that student relationships come first, and everything is second.

Jamie received her Bachelor of Arts in both Spanish and Mass Media from Houston Baptist University and her Master of Education from Texas A&M University. Jamie has facilitated professional development at the district level as well as broader audiences like the Technology & Curriculum Conference (TCCA) in Aldine ISD and at the Region 6

Education Service Center. She lives in Texas with her husband, a middle schooler, a high schooler, and a forever daughter who is now a teacher herself.

THE IMPACT OF POSITIVE RELATIONSHIPS

Clara J. Alaniz

What does current research say about how relationships impact student achievement?

Think about your time as a student in elementary, middle, or high school. Recall the name of your favorite teacher. What are some words or phrases you might use to describe this teacher? It is very likely that this teacher was kind, compassionate, sincere, and/or engaging.

Now, consider how this inspiring teacher made you feel. When you walked into that classroom, did you feel valued, loved, and important? Were you actively engaged in the classroom activities? Were you eager to show her/him your assignment or something you created for class? Did this teacher have high expectations of you? Did you make good grades in that class? It is very probable that your answers to the last five questions were all yes.

The likely reason this teacher stands out to you is because she/he took the time to get to know you as both a student and an individual. That positive relationship was built on trust and compassion which was used to establish personalized goals and set high, achievable expectations for you. This teacher wanted you to be successful in that class and sincerely believed that you could rise to the occasion.

On the contrary, now consider a teacher you did not particularly like. What are some words or phrases you might use to describe this individual? How did she/he make you feel? Were you eager to produce high quality work and put forth extra effort? It is very likely that you felt unwelcome the second you walked into that class. It is possible that you felt this teacher did not care about you. It is also possible that you felt no urgency when completing assignments or participating in class activities. If this teacher had high expectations of you and believed you could succeed, it was likely not made clear. Or worse, this teacher made you feel as if you'd never succeed and did not believe in you.

The positive relationships educators build with students make a tremendous and lasting impact. Research also shows that the relationships educators have with each other also make a positive impact in the classroom.

John Hattie is a professor at the University of Melbourne in Australia. In the early 1980s, he began his research into various indicators that impact student achievement, both in positive and negative ways. Decades of additional research has led to similar indicators that regularly make an impact in classrooms. The statistics in Hattie's research was measured in effect size to show the level of impact for various indicators. An indicator with a high effect size made a larger impact in learning. In 2018, the following effect sizes were found in Hattie's research:

Indicator	Effect Size
Collective Teacher Efficacy	1.57
Teacher Estimates of Achievement	1.29
Learning Goals vs. No Goals	0.68
Clear Goal Intentions	0.48
Students Feeling Disliked	-0.19

COLLECTIVE TEACHER EFFICACY

Teacher efficacy can be defined as the belief of one's own ability to promote positive change for students. It is my hope that all teachers feel they are effective in their work to bring about positive learning outcomes.

Collective teacher efficacy is a group's beliefs about their collective ability to promote successful learning outcomes for students. It is also the indicator with the highest effect size in all of Hattie's research. Collective efficacy is when all members of a team share the belief that they are capable of making positive changes for students. We, as educators, must collectively believe in our team's abilities and skills to support learning.

In my job, I am fortunate to work on a digital learning team with 3 other women. They are each skilled in their own ways and I am deeply grateful for the brilliant contributions they each make to our team. I recognize my self-efficacy and believe that I make a positive impact on student achievement. However, when I think about my team and our collective action to promote positive change, I believe that we are unstoppable and can handle anything!

Leah Heerema, Lilly Jensby, Fern Johnson, and I are the only members of a digital learning team that supports over 50,000 students and

7,000 staff members. That ratio does not slow us down one bit! Our team thoroughly believes in our skillful ability to support teachers and students in engaging, innovative, digital learning environments. It is important to note that our strong, respectful, professional relationship is the reason why we are able to build and maintain collective efficacy.

Consider your own self-efficacy. What are the ways in which you are making meaningful, impactful changes in the lives of students? Consider your team's collective efficacy. No matter the size of the team, do the staff members all believe in the team's collective ability to make a positive impact? Are the team members contributing to a respectful professional relationship? To read more about this topic, I strongly recommend the book, *Collective Efficacy*, by Jenni Donohoo for its helpful suggestions and plans on how to build and maintain collective efficacy.

TEACHER ESTIMATES OF ACHIEVEMENT, LEARNING GOALS, AND CLEAR GOAL INTENTIONS

One way of improving collective efficacy, while also working toward learning targets, is for teachers to establish challenging expectations and goals for students. It is true that a culture and a climate conducive to growth mindset are helpful in supporting student achievement. But, as research shows, teachers' hopes of what the students can achieve should be paired with the fundamental belief that they can do it.

When considering what a student can accomplish, a teacher will rely on her/his knowledge of that student. In order to set learning expectations, a teacher will evaluate the learning styles, skills, and previous knowledge of the student. The instructional strategies and methods selected to reach the learning goals are dependent upon what the teacher knows about the student. Working with the student to set learning goals should be part of this process and those goals should be clearly communicated so that the student understands the expectations. However, none of this can be done if there is not a strong relationship between the teacher and student. The teacher needs to understand the learner and express a sincere belief that the student can meet his/her goals. The learner needs to feel valued and respected by the teacher in order to maintain a positive attitude and actively work toward the goals.

All the teachers on a team/campus could use their collective knowledge to establish estimates of achievement, create goals, and clearly communicate their intentions. Then, the students would understand that high expectations are shared across every subject and teacher.

Think back to your favorite teacher. You likely felt there were high expectations in that class and your teacher set those expectations based on what she/he knew about you. Your teacher understood you and how you learned. She/he was able to estimate what you could achieve and set a learning goal. Because you knew this teacher cared deeply for you, it is very likely that you worked hard and exceeded expectations.

STUDENTS FEELING DISLIKED

Unfortunately, there are too many stories about what happens when a student feels disliked. Students feel unwelcome in those classrooms and might not feel the need to engage in class. Students are quick to pick up on these unpleasant feelings and, according to Hattie's research, that has a profoundly negative impact on achievement.

If a teacher does not develop a positive relationship with a student, it will be very difficult to establish estimates of achievement. It will be even more difficult to set relevant goals and clearly communicate their intentions with the student. The only aspect the student will clearly understand is that she/he feels disliked. The student will feel as though the teacher does not believe in her/him and that there is a low level of expectation.

From a personal perspective, I felt that more teachers disliked me than liked me. Throughout my many years as a student, (pre-k to high school, a Bachelor's degree, and two Master's degrees) there were only a handful of educators who took the time to get to know me. Being disliked became my norm and I got into the habit of working hard to meet the goals I set for myself. I also got used to not having relationships with my teachers and administrators because many of them expressed their uncertainty in my ability to achieve. I did very well in school and always scored high on assignments and exams. I was an honor student, but I absolutely hated being at school.

I am glad I exceeded my own expectations, but could I have done even more if I had been encouraged by my teachers? Could I have learned even more if my personal goals were better aligned to instructional goals? Those questions are partly why I became an educator. It is my passion to make school an effective, engaging, inclusive place to learn and that is reliant upon building positive relationships with all members of our learning community.

"Be who you needed when you were younger" is a mantra I keep framed in my office. When I was younger, I needed my teachers to build positive relationships with me and believe in me. Every day, I work to be the educator I needed back then and I hope I never let them down.

REFERENCES

J. Donahoo. (2016). *Collective Efficacy: How Educators' Beliefs Impact Student Learning.* Corwin.

J. Hattie, K. Zierer. (2018). *10 Mindframes for Visible Learning: Teaching for Success.* Routledge.

Clara J. Alaniz

ABOUT THE AUTHOR

Clara J. Alaniz is a fifth generation Texan and has been a digital learning specialist since 2001. She also served as an elementary school teacher. Clara is a certified Principal and certified Technology/IT Director. She is an ISTE Certified Educator and serves as the Advocacy Chair for the ISTE Education Leaders PLN. In 2016, Clara was selected to join the Technical Working Group that refreshed the ISTE Standards for Educators. In 2019, she was selected to join the Technical Working Group to refresh the ISTE Standards for Coaches. Clara is a Google Certified Trainer and a Google Certified Educator, Level 1 and 2.

Her husband, Marcos, is a firefighter and they have two sons, Evan and Ian. Clara is a voracious reader, avid sewist, and world traveler.

MINDFUL, NOT MIND FULL
Kate Weber

Breathing mindfulness into our classrooms benefits us all

In this chapter you will learn how utilizing mindfulness will have unending effects into your teaching practice, classroom community, and overall school culture.

THE BEGINNING

When approached about how to begin the journey to mindfulness with students, I often ask teachers if they are prepared to do the work themselves. Mindfulness will only be effective and authentic if it is adopted as a mindset of the person delivering it. Teachers, you need to do the work. We all do. Mindfulness requires focus, presence, and attentiveness to what is in front of us and this is pretty much the polar opposite of how traditional educational systems are set up. Leaving everyone in its system frazzled, broken and frantically searching for something that will 'fix' the problem. The 'problem' is not a system filled with broken, frazzled, and frantic students and teachers, but it is the system that is broken, frazzled, and frantic itself.

Stress is part of the full human experience—we will never lead a stress-free life. This is something that also needs some work in schools—students may not be exposed to having to deal with stress at all so they largely have no coping skills when faced with adversity. It is important to know how to deal with stress healthily and it may be the job of schools to create opportunities for learning about healthy stress and how to manage it. When stress becomes persistent, it tips over into toxic stress. Toxic stress occurs when the demands of your life consistently outpace your ability to cope with those demands. Toxic stress in our schools creates problems for both students and teachers. For students, toxic stress can lead to attention, mood, and sleep struggles. Prolonged exposure to toxic stress during childhood impacts mental and physical health for the duration of one's life. When exposed to prolonged stress, teachers decrease in productivity, focus and eventually escalate into anxiety, depression, and burnout. When we are exposed to toxic stress over a long period, it creates a fight or flight response in the body making it next to impossible to focus or learn. Our bodies are doing what they are hardwired to do in our automatic response system, attempting to keep us alert and ready to respond at any moment.

We have to stop blaming teachers for their burnout and own up to the idea that our system is the one that is burnt out. We have to stop wondering where the rise in mental health issues are coming from and ask some hard questions about how we promote mental health in our schools, or conversely how we promote things that create the conditions for a mental health crisis to flourish in the first place. The rise of standardized testing, rigorous coursework, punitive grading, huge class sizes, underfunded schools, pressures from parents and administration, worrying about students, and making it through to the next day are just some of the things that may be creating the conditions for mental health breaks in both teachers and students. Just because this is how we have done it for decades and decades does not mean it needs to, or should, continue this way any longer. We know better and now we have the tools to help all students and ourselves to be better.

So what is mindfulness? At its most basic definition mindfulness is simply awareness. Paying attention. Noticing. Slowing Down. Accepting one's present reality while acknowledging feelings, thoughts, ideas, and bodily sensations. Mindfulness is not exotic or new. It is something we naturally do, especially as children, but we are usually distracted or conditioned to fall into patterns of mindlessness as we grow older. We learn that to be efficient and successful, we need to be constantly moving and hustling to make those things happen. We replace presence with to-do lists and achievements to tick off. We become distracted from our current condition by thinking about what needs to be done in the future.

Distractions are everywhere, both internal and external, while the most notable of those external distractions would be an attachment to technology and social media. We take, on average, 23,000 breaths a day. This is a staggering number, but how often are you consciously aware of your breathing? Think about how much time you spend on your phone a day and consider if you are even aware of your breathing while you are scrolling or answering emails. Likely, not very aware at all. It wasn't until I began my investigation into breathwork, did I learn how to use my breath as a tool for self-regulation, to breathe through the panic, anxiety, and stress. In teaching these techniques to my students, I learned that most of them have little to no understanding of how their breath and parasympathetic nervous systems function together.

I like the idea of mindfulness as a space—a small sliver of space between me and the things in my life that bombard me daily: teaching, family, momming, friends, grading, classroom chaos, etc. When I began adding mindfulness into my daily life, it began as meditation—two minutes was about all I could manage. Meditation is one way to develop mindfulness, but there are many ways to achieve awareness. When I began using meditation as a therapeutic technique, I had this feeling of coming home after being away for a long time. It was like I was coming home, stepping into familiar surroundings and feeling at ease. In my classroom, I rarely use the word meditation because it usually turns kids off in my experience. Instead, I say 'breathing', 'sitting' or 'being.'

There are many reasons we would want more awareness in our schools, and the research behind mindfulness is starting to become more widely known and used to help apply mindfulness to improve the overall cultures of schools. Here are a few of the reasons for using mindfulness in our schools is necessary:

- Being stuck in the past and fretting about the future leaves students no time to be in the present moment. Helping them come back to where they are will only allow them to absorb what you are teaching even more.
- Taking small mindful breaks will help them self-regulate, find their level again, and be able to focus more intently during the day. Many studies show improvements in attention in those who regularly use mindfulness.
- Mindful kids are happier kids! Students that feel happier during the day are more likely to believe learning/school to be a good thing—helping drive attendance, relationship building and overall well-being. Mindfulness has been associated with emotional regulation and it creates changes in the brain that correspond to being less reactive. This means those who

practice mindfulness are better able to engage in tasks even when their emotions are elevated.
- Happier and calmer kids are also less likely to harm themselves or others around them, improving the overall culture and safety of your class or school. Someone who uses mindfulness regularly is more likely to help others in need and often have a greater level of self-compassion. Studies find that mindfulness reduces feelings of stress and improves anxiety and distress when in stressful social settings.

It is time our education system steps up to look after the whole child. We've had many conversations about whole child education, social-emotional regulation, but I am unsure if this is changing. Yet. When we start the journey into holistic education, it means we are attempting to care for ALL needs of our learners, those needs beyond academics and attendance. If we can aid students to develop their mental fitness and resilience, it will become a lifelong skill transferable into the rest of their dynamic lives. Plus, adding mindfulness breaks or activities into your classroom will let your students know you care about them, not just their brains, but all of their hearts too! Students who feel cared about are more likely to listen to their instructions, show up to class and be better behaved because they also learn to care about you!

Another captivating piece of information surrounding the use of mindfulness practices in school is that when teachers learn mindfulness they not only reap personal benefits such as reduced stress and burnout, but their schools do as well. Shifting school culture and climate by implementing personal mindfulness practices seems like a worthwhile investment for districts and schools. This will help keep teachers in the building, reduce the need for substitutes, keep teachers in their positions longer, and reduce hiring and teacher turnover rates. Teachers who learned mindfulness reported greater efficacy in doing their jobs and had more emotionally supportive classrooms and better classroom organization.

Mindfulness impacts our brains in both their functioning and potentially their structure. The amygdala, which reacts to strong emotions especially fear, following mindfulness training is less activated and has less gray matter density. This means that our 'triggered' emotional states are less touchy when we have a structured mindfulness practice. The hippocampus, which is critical for learning and memory and helps regulate the amygdala, is MORE active and has MORE gray matter density following mindfulness practice. The prefrontal cortex, responsible for self-regulation and associated with maturity, is more activated following mindfulness training. As a simple practice, with all of the benefits pointing towards implementing this in our classrooms, the question remains: HOW do we do this?

I had the benefit of having some of my Social Studies students filter into my Yoga for Wellness option in the afternoon and this is where I was truly able to see mindfulness making a huge difference in their everyday lives. Every day we would move, breathe, and write. Simple, but so powerful. Mindfulness was the glue that held it all together and by laying inquiry into their experience, they became more self-aware, better at regulating their emotional struggles, and more resilient in the classroom. The best example I have of this was when I was supervising final exams, I noticed that not just one or two, but MOST of the yogis I had in the afternoon were closing their eyes, placing a hand on their heart and closing their eyes during moments of duress on their exams. The win was that they were utilizing these tools because they were aware enough of needing them in the first place.

We don't know what we don't know until we know it and this is precisely the purpose of mindfulness—once we start our journey towards awareness we may be tempted to be angry with ourselves for past mistakes or burnout. We must be loving and compassionate towards ourselves because all we can do is seek to learn more and deepen our awareness of ourselves as we move forward in life. This is important to help your students with as well, as they will feel like their past selves were 'less than' or that they 'failed.' I have seen this happen with a number of my students during mindfulness exploration and it requires compassionate conversation and communication. Seeking to fix the past will only create more suffering. All we can do is move forward to a better, more aware future.

There are many ways to create mindfulness in our lives and classrooms, but the outcome is always the same: presence, awareness, acceptance. This can be found through meditation, play, walking, writing, dancing, and moving, The biggest part of mindfulness that we need to remember is that we, as educators, need to invest in doing the work ourselves. Mindfulness can only be authentic in our classrooms, and therefore long-lasting if it is embraced as a foundational shift away from the frazzled and frantic pace of our traditional education system to one of presence, joy, and accepting what is instead of wishing for what could be. I will give you some simple and practical ideas to take into your life and classroom in the next section of this chapter—try them out yourself so you can deliver them in an authentic way to your students.

MINDFULNESS FOR TEACHERS & STUDENTS

Simple, but not always easy, the following activities can be the beginning of a day/lesson, or during times of stress (exams, staff meetings, parent meetings, etc.) and even used as full learning experiences for both health and physical education lessons.

ABOVE ALL, BE GENTLE WITH YOURSELF. This work takes practice and it is not something that can be cultivated without frequency. Approach your thoughts as friends and not enemies— your brain is not something to control but might be something we can train. I highly encourage anyone I work with, teachers and students, to write in a journal as part of their mindfulness practice. Usually, it is most effective AFTER one of the following exercises or any sort of mindfulness exercises (walking, dancing, meditating, coloring, etc.) Write about what you felt, experienced, struggled with or felt success at. Also free to write about ANYTHING you need to process. Don't be worried about 'sounding' right or writing something perfectly. Many of the times I write after meditating it will look more like a messy map of ideas and words, but it is what works for me.

Writing, in and of itself, is a mindfulness exercise and it is deeply reflective. For teachers, myself included, this is more than just reflective practice—it is a deeply personal reflection about ME as a person not just ME as a teacher. If I take care of myself, my full self not just my teacher self, I will be a more effective teacher in the long run and likely find joy in my career more frequently. Mindfulness only works when we do the work!

Mindfulness has two expressions: everyday or trait mindfulness and formal sitting mindfulness. Through formal practice, one can develop trait mindfulness, but it is really about keeping a thread of continuity through your formal practice—even if it is 10 breaths. We can't spend time with the mind unless we TAKE time to do it. Even though a formal sitting or meditation practice seems daunting, it is often our minds 'tricking' us into believing it is scarier than it is. When we know the benefits of mindfulness are real and tangible in our daily lives and will have lasting effects on our relationships and overall joy in life, we can justify 5-10 minutes of formal practice. Something that helps me get through this resistance is asking myself "If I sit still and breathe for five minutes, what is the worst thing that could happen?" and usually I can't argue with that, so I submit and do the practice. Often one of the best strategies is to carve out a time that works for you in your regular day such as before work, lunchtime, and after work. Maybe you only sit for two minutes, but eventually, that can expand to maybe 5 minutes each time. Our mindfulness muscle only works for us when we work it regularly.

Suggestions for Success:

- Try sitting up or supported against a wall. Sitting in a chair is great too—just make sure your feet are planted firmly on the ground. We don't want to give signals to the body for sleep by laying down, but you have to decide what will work best for your practice!
- Concentrate, but don't focus too hard that you pull yourself away from the mindfulness practice. Relax! There is no wrong way to concentrate or practice mindfulness. Be gentle with

yourself—especially if this is a brand new practice for you. It will take time to build up the mental fitness required for sustained focus.
- Have fun with it! There will be so many things you can do to gain awareness these are just some starting suggestions, not a one-size-fits-all solution.
- Remember, there is no 'right' or 'wrong' way to do this practice! Trying to stop all thoughts in the mind is impossible —that is what your brain is supposed to do! Meet your thoughts like friends, not enemies, and see how your practice will become more comfortable.

A FEW WORDS ABOUT BREATH

Breathing exercises require just that: breathing. This is something we do every day, but largely as a side product of our day to day life - rarely acknowledged or improved upon. We take, on average, 23,000 breaths a day (Schriger, 2007), so yes...it is important to help students learn the power their breath holds at helping them find calm, focus and presence throughout their day. It is likely something that we, as educators, aren't aware of enough during our day either.

Our breath works in connection with our parasympathetic nervous system to determine if we are under stress or not. Your body might be in a low-grade stress response just because of how you are breathing. Shallow breathing, breathing that sits just on the top of the chest, is associated with stress, panic, and anxiety. Whereas breathing low and slow into the chest and then belly with exhales slowly out of the mouth or nostrils, allows our bodies to receive signals we are not being attacked by a large animal. When our bodies are under stress for long periods, our systems start to malfunction and deteriorate. Stomachaches, headaches, and heart conditions are all linked to long-term stress in the body. Breathing is our way to take the power back.

During any of the meditations or activities, the breath needs to be slow and low - send into the belly and not just into the chest. We are trying to lengthen inhales and exhales to improve the quality of our breath. This takes work, so be gentle with yourself when you are first starting. Like anything worthy of our time, it requires some effort! The more you practice, the easier, and more beneficial these practices become.

HEART & BELLY BREATH

This breathing activity includes physical touch which can be soothing during times of distress or distraction. Also, it encourages a deep breath into the belly which allows us to break the pattern of breathing shallow and into our chest only (this is usually where we breath when we are panicking or anxious).

1. Sit on a mat or in a chair with both feet flat on the floor. Close your eyes. Allow your body to settle into your chosen position, adjusting or shifting if needed.
2. Bring your right hand on your belly and your left hand over your heart.
3. Pay attention to the rise and fall of your chest hand and belly hand.
4. Inhale, feeling the heart hand rise followed by belly hand, and on the exhale, feeling the belly hand fall followed by heart hand. Noticing how this breathing connects to the natural rhythm and movement of your breath.
5. Take five cycles of breath this way (or more!).
6. Feel your breath as it enters your mouths or nostrils. Noticing how it is cool as it enters your body on the inhale and how it is warm as it exits your body on the exhale.
7. Take five cycles of breath this way (or more!).
8. Next, see if you can hear your breath as you gently inhale and gently exhale.
9. Take five cycles of breath this way (or more!).
10. Next, see if you can get so quiet that you can hear your heartbeat. Pay attention to what you feel and hear.
11. Bring both hands to the heart center, gently opening the eyes and smile.

BALLOON BELLY BREATH

This breathing technique is particularly useful when trying to coax the breath out of the chest (anxious breathing pattern) and into the belly.

1. Sit on a mat or in a chair with both feet flat on the floor. This meditation is also really great when done laying down. Close your eyes. Allow your body to settle into your chosen position, adjusting or shifting if needed.
2. Visualize (or do this demonstration with a balloon with your students) a balloon inflating and then slowly getting the air released out of it.
3. Place both hands on the belly, around the belly button.
4. Imagine that there is a balloon in your belly and as you inhale you are slowly filling up that balloon. Focus on your belly expanding outwards.
5. Exhale slowly through your mouth (sighing if that feels good), letting all the air out of your balloon. Focus on your belly falling inwards.
6. On your next inhale, try to count to 4 as you breathe in, holding for a few counts at the top, and then exhale to a count of 4 as you breathe out through the mouth.
7. Keep this counting going, seeing if you can increase it to counts of 6 or more.
8. Bring both hands to the heart center, open the eyes and smile.

OCEAN BREATHING

The visualization of a wave rolling into the body and then out is a soothing and calming technique useful for moments of stress. Great before and exam, meeting or perhaps just to gain more presence during a small moment in your day.

1. Begin by finding a comfortable position to sit—supported by a chair or wall works great too. Take some time to get as comfortable as you can before you begin.

2. Bring the right hand to the belly and the left hand to the heart.
3. Inhale to the heart and then deepen the inhale to the belly. Pause
4. Exhale, let the belly fall and then the chest fall as you exhale. Pause.
5. Inhale, chest and belly rise. Pause.
6. Exhale, belly and chest fall. Pause.
7. Let the wave of your breath pass into the chest and belly and then roll out of the belly and then out of the chest.
8. Repeat 4-5 times.
9. Let go of controlling the breath take a deep inhale and then exhale through the mouth. Bring the hands to the heart center, blink the eyes open and smile.

REFERENCES

Schriger, D.L. (2007) Approach to the patient with abnormal vital signs. Goldman L, Ausiello D. Cecil Textbook of Medicine. 23rd ed. Philadelphia, Pa:Saunders Elsevier; 2007:chap 7.

Kate Weber

ABOUT THE AUTHOR

I am a passionate high school teacher, yoga teacher, writer and mindfulness enthusiast who lives and works in Northern Alberta. I have become deeply invested in the wellbeing of those who work in and alongside the education system and I am convinced that unless we dig deep and do the work ourselves, nothing with change.

I work in a high school redesign project that takes away semesterised and streamed core classes, and replaces it with a free flowing full year relationship based 'pod' of students and teachers. As one of four "core" teachers, I team teach and integrate the other subjects (as well as mindfulness, yoga and fine arts) into my social studies teaching. I am in love with the relationships I am able to build with students during this two year cycle through grade 10 and grade 11. I have worked in this "pod" system for four years and could never see myself returning to a regular traditional style system. I feel very lucky to have the opportunity to work creatively and with autonomy in this system.

Two years ago I was inspired to create a few new programs and classes within my school to promote student wellness as well as professional development for teachers struggling with burnout, frustration and mental health issues. This resulted in a yoga for wellness class as well as a PD training opportunity called "RADeducators." Since then I have written a short book, recorded audio meditations and launched a website to promote these things (www.kateweber.ca)

It is my hope that one day my students, colleagues and friends have an educational experience that embeds their wellness and makes it a top priority. I hope to leave anyone I meet feeling inspired, lit up, deeply loved and supported. I am so grateful you are here, exploring this site, and allowing my beautiful dream to become a reality. THANK YOU!

"THAT MIGHT WORK WITH SOME STUDENTS..."

Kimber Johnston

Don't be fooled -- this stuff works with ALL students, some just might need a little more scaffolding.

JUST TRY IT!

Why is it that educators who are passionate about and supportive of their students fall into the trap of saying "Maybe **your** kids can do that," or "That won't work with **my** students"? Are we afraid of trying and failing at something new? Are we trying to protect our students from failure?

Instead of "That might word for your students," let's practice saying, "How can I make that work for my students?"

It can be overwhelming when you're faced with an educator who has amazing student work samples, and utter confidence that you can get the same results with your students. I've been there. I've also been the overly enthusiastic educator effusing at another teacher and spotting the deer-in-headlights look in their eyes.

The thing is, when we're busy evangelizing about how great something will be in your classroom, we don't actually expect your results to look exactly like our results. Our results probably didn't even look like our results when we first started. What we're excited about is the learning. We're excited about the fact that our students got excited. We're excited that something worked for us and our kids.

Your students are your students. You do know your students' needs. But instead of dismissing those enthusiastic folks as unrealistic, tell them about your students. Ask them about strategies. And sometimes, they, we, I might be stumped. But the discourse that follows will be gold. It might be just what you need to provide the inspiration for how to implement, not a cookie-cutter of another teacher's idea, but a version of an idea that will help your students get to the deep learning we're all striving for. As time goes on, I'm getting better at asking myself (and other educators) what the essential conditions are of their project or approach, why it works to deepen learning, and how they accommodate students who learn differently. I'm also building a bigger toolbox of ways to adapt and modify instruction so I can confidently introduce cool new stuff to my students without worrying that I'll let them down.

And when it's your turn to be the effusively gushing, overly excited edu-vangelist because you're so stoked about how your students took off with a certain project or approach? Watch for that deer-in-headlights look. Start asking questions about the other teachers' students, so you can help them envision how it will look for their kids.

We all want our students to grow and succeed. But we need to practice what we try to instill in them -- take risks, be resilient. We can be great models for them, and they will reap the benefits not only of seeing our words in action but also of the innovative learning experiences they'll have the opportunity to explore.

YEAH, BUT...

"But my students can't read" -- use video and audio support to let students experience the content and instructions, then let them flow with multiple means of expression for their deliverables. Make sure students know they are always welcome to use things like voice typing or dictation to express themselves in writing. Offer Thin Slides, Comic Strips, Sketch-Noting, Flipgrid, or Screencast video responses instead of traditional text-heavy artifacts of learning. Allow mixed-media deliverables -- some students feel more comfortable hand-writing or sketching a portion of their work, then snapshotting it and remixing it in Slides or weVideo or Scratch or... the options are pretty limitless, but choose a handful of choices to start, and go with it.

"But my students don't like to write" -- use multi-modal deliverables that use images or video to convey the larger portions of students' message, with text captions for clarity. Many of the same suggestions above will appeal to students who have dysgraphia, who have difficulty expressing their ideas in text, or who are otherwise reluctant writers. Don't let your students off the hook, but focus on the ideas instead of the medium.

"But my students don't speak English" -- use visual support to augment your instructions, while providing Google Translate and allowing students to brainstorm and ideate in their home language. Scaffold with crowd-sourced word banks and sentence frames, then allow deliverables similar to those above.

"But my students' behaviors are too extreme for that type of project" -- If your students are familiar with very structured classroom routines, work your way into voice and choice a little at a time. Readers/Writers Workshop, Daily 5, and other systems have great instructional support for building students' stamina to work independently. Chunk the project into bite-sized pieces that are easily modeled. For students whose self-regulation skills truly will not allow for less structured time, think about the type of scaffolds and milestones you can put in place to support them while still allowing them to stretch beyond their comfort zone a bit at a time. Things that might be unimaginable when you first begin will seem like no big deal by the end of the year -- incremental progress adds up!

"But my students would never be interested in something like that" -- Most often, our students get excited because we are excited.

But if you really believe that your unflagging enthusiasm is still not enough to get things rolling, modify the project to include something you know your students like, even if you only touch on it tangentially. Our students want to make meaning of what we are asking them to do. We can make it easier for them by building in opportunities for connection.

"But I'll never have time for that" -- the thing about big, time-consuming projects is that they almost always thoroughly cover several standards. Instead of thinking of the project or approach as yet another thing to do in addition to teaching all your standards, use it as the way you'll teach your standards. Recoup the instructional time you were planning to spend to teach those standards using another approach. For the occasions when it's still the case that you won't have time, scale the project to fit the time you do have. You might be surprised how much you can do once your students get familiar with your new approach.

"But it's scary" -- Yep. And just as we want our students to be courageous with their learning, you can be too.

I have a colleague who is now a close friend. When I met her, she was pretty new to teaching, it was her first year teaching at my school, and she was going to be teaching a class of students with learning differences. When I bowled her over with my enthusiasm and ideas for her students, she took a deep breath and dove in. She is in year 3 at that site, and her students consistently perform at a high level, doing inquiry projects, writing screenplays, producing videos and art projects. Their work is on par with what might be expected of "typically developing" students. My friend was willing to step far out of her comfort zone and she was transparent about it with her students. Her students have developed agency, resiliency, and a willingness to be more courageous with their own learning. And she has grown into a cheerleader and mentor for others -- including me!

READY OR NOT

I hope you'll dive in the next time someone shares something super cool that seems out of reach or frightening to try with your students. Do think about your students' needs. Then, figure out what you need to do to help your students be successful with a new approach or project, or a new kind of learning. The beauty part is, it gets easier each time -- you'll have more confidence and tools to make it work, and your students will be more confident in their abilities as well!

Kimber Johnston

ABOUT THE AUTHOR

Kimber serves as the weCreate Director at Shattuck St. Mary's School in Forest City, Malaysia, and has a strong background in American education, including serving as the Director of Technology at a K-8 school specializing in students with learning differences. She has her

MEd in Learning Design and Leadership and is a Google Certified Educator and Trainer. She loves working with students and educators to integrate technology into teaching and learning, and believes technology can be life-changing for students as it improves their access knowledge and helps them share their ideas.

GOING GRADELESS
Melissa-Ann Pero

When children are young, they are sponges. They watch and listen and repeat sounds and words and actions. They are constantly re-evaluating their surroundings and reimagining their abilities. They are learning. And they learn because they are curious. Amazing things are everywhere, and children yearn to be a part of all the incredible things happening around them. They learn to crawl and walk, to use a fork and use a spoon, to hold a pencil and hold a conversation. And they do all of this with the sole incentive to learn things, to become a part of the world that is ever-growing before them.

And then those children get to formal school settings. At some point, these children who have been so eager to learn things just for the sake of soaking it all in, are told that learning things comes with labels. Children begin to see their learning on a scale, and they (and the education system in general) categorize themselves in accordance with their perception of that scale. Children get pushed into categories like "failure" and "basic" and "average" and "proficient."

There is undoubtedly a culture of high-stakes grades and pressure on scores in the field of education, beginning with admissions testing for elite private pre-schools all the way to and past the SATs and GREs needed for college and graduate admissions. This culture produces a LOT of pressure about what these scores mean in relationship to learner success—on students, parents, and teachers.

As a current member of all THREE of these categories, I've realized how much these categories and pressures have hindered students' confidence, creativity, and eagerness to learn. My research has led me to a movement that needs more voices and much more support—a movement that has the potential to change the way students learn, teachers teach, and parents advocate.

We eliminate grades and encourage children's love of learning through feedback.

For some of you, your reaction is assuredly, "Did you say get rid of grades? How is that possible? How do you measure success? Knowledge? Learning?" These are great questions, and the people considering and implementing gradelessness, they have the answers. Or at least the beginnings of them.

On Jan 10, 2018, educator and author of the book Hack Learning Mark Barnes[1] wrote a commentary for Education Week[2] giving a rationale for removing grades. The ultimate outcome, he says, is that "students would become independent learners, driven by curiosity and inspiration." And isn't that what we want our students to become? Curious and inspired, driven to continue to learn?

There are many ways to begin working through how to go gradeless in the midst of a system that requires scores to rate achievement and success. Check out Alfie Kohn[3] and his research on our country's fixation on grades. Research posts at Teachers Going Gradeless[4] and their Twitter account @TG2Chat.[5] Research ways to incorporate feedback as an evaluation standard using single-point rubrics, and focus on standards and skills mastery as an evaluation tool.

Children begin in the world with an inherent love of curiosity, exploration, and learning. Our job as educators is to foster the insatiable need children have to want to know. Real learning is about the love of the adventure curiosity leads us on. Imagine what could happen if we eliminate the pressure of grades and scores and just join in on the adventure?

∽

Melissa-Ann Pero

Melissa-Ann Pero is a former high school English teacher and yearbook advisor currently working as a staff developer for the Lincoln Intermediate Unit in New Oxford, PA. She has been a presenter and coordinator at various district, area, and state conferences in Pennsylvania. She is a actively involved in the Pennsylvania Association for Educational Communications and Technology and the Pennsylvania Teachers Advisory Committee. She is also a Keystone Technology Innovator and a bit of an edtech junkie. She's excited to be a part of the education conversation as a teacher and a learner and is working to complete her Doctorate in Curriculum and Instruction. She's always looking to grow her PLC so please follow her on Twitter @melannpero.

EDUCATORS, GET COMFORTABLE WITH THE UNCOMFORTABLE: DYSLEXIA

Winifred A. Winston (@winningwithwinifred)

Without the proper remediation, most dyslexics are often left feeling inadequate, less than, stupid, lack confidence, have low self-esteem, or may suffer from depression. This follows them into adulthood and into the workplace.

BUT FIRST ...WHAT IS DYSLEXIA?

According to the Mayo Clinic, dyslexia is a learning disorder that involves difficulty reading due to problems identifying speech sounds and learning how they relate to letter words (decoding). It affects areas of the brain that process language.

EDUCATE

Learn all you can about dyslexia and the science of reading. Unfortunately, most educators do not learn the science of reading while earning their undergraduate teaching degree and therefore, lack adequate training to recognize and treat students who struggle to learn how to read. It's imperative that you learn how to identify dyslexia, how to treat dyslexia, and what interventions work for dyslexics.

School psychologists can identify characteristics of dyslexia by conducting an educational evaluation as well as a cognitive evaluation. Most school districts will say they do not "diagnose" dyslexia, that's why I'm carefully using the term, "identify." However, formal testing of reading, language, and writing skills conducted by a licensed educational psychologist or neurologist are able to diagnose dyslexia. Please note, there are other trained and certified educators/reading specialists who are able to confirm dyslexia as well. For the sake of this piece, I want to focus on staff that teachers are most familiar with and who will help determine eligibility for special education services during an IEP meeting. According to Dyslexia Help at the University of Michigan, the following assessments are used to diagnose dyslexia:

- Rapid Automatic Naming/Rapid Automatic Stimulus (RAN/RAS)
- Test of Auditory Processing Skills (TAPS)
- Test of Early Written Language (TEWL)
- Test of Pragmatic Language (TOPL)
- Test of Written Language -4 (TOWL-4)
- Test of Written Spelling – 5 (TWS-5)

- Woodock Reading Mastery Test (WRMT)
- Word Test

According to the International Dyslexia Association, multi-sensory structured literacy is used to treat dyslexia. Structured literacy (SL) approaches emphasize highly explicit and systematic teaching of all important components (foundational skills and higher-level literacy skills) of literacy. Foundational skills include decoding and spelling, while higher-level literacy skills include reading comprehension and written expression.

Lastly, research has shown that there are several reading interventions that work for dyslexics if taught with fidelity. Some of those programs include Orton – Gillingham, OG, The Barton Reading and Spelling System, and The Wilson Reading System (Tier 3) just to name a few.

Did you know: According to the National Institutes of Health, dyslexia is identifiable with 92% accuracy at the age of 5.5?

EMPOWER

Arm yourself with the tools to address dyslexia in your classroom. Gain a grasp on what interventions your school has in place and what accommodations are proven to work to help struggling readers in the classroom.

Warning signs of dyslexia might include the following:

- Unable to remember sight words
- Sloppy handwriting (dysgraphia)
- Very poor spelling
- Unable to remember math facts (counting money is very challenging)
- Unable to recall words when speaking (you'll hear a lot of pauses, umm, and you knows)
- Directionality (difficultly remembering left from right)

According to Understood.org, some accommodations for dyslexia in the classroom include:

- Post visual schedules and also read them out loud
- Provide colored strips or bookmarks to help focus on a line of text when reading
- Provide extra time for reading and writing in the classroom
- Give the student multiple opportunities to read the same text
- Pre-teach new concepts and vocabulary
- Provide advance organizers to help the student follow along during a lesson
- Use visual or audio support to help the student understand written materials in the lecture
- Give step-by-step directions and read written instructions out loud
- Highlight key words and ideas on worksheets for the student to read first

Did you know: Dyslexia is the #1 learning disability in the classroom and falls under the category Special Learning Disability (SLD) with the IDEA when determining eligibility for special education services.

EQUIP

As a classroom teacher you should feel empowered to help make change at the local, state, and federal level so all children can learn how to read. You are the best person to supply the necessary evidence of what works in the classroom and what does not work. In addition, you know first hand what you did not learn in college while preparing to become a teacher. Many local school districts are left to fill the knowledge gap left open by colleges of education and your voice would be instrumental in change needed at the higher education level.

For support in how to get your voice heard, join an organization such as Decoding Dyslexia, a parent-led grassroots movement of educators, parents, and related service providers who want to raise awareness about struggling readers and dyslexia.

Did you know: 36 States enacted reading and/or dyslexia screening laws; is your state one of them?

In conclusion, I hope these 3 quick steps will raise educator awareness about dyslexia and methods to help struggling readers. As a k-12, classroom teacher, I was not provided the necessary tools to help my high school students who struggled to read or who struggled with comprehension. While working in higher education, I'd share with my students and adult learners, you are the CEO of your career. Don't wait for an employer, and in this case, the school district, to map out your professional development. Educate, empower, and equip yourself with the necessary tools to become a successful educator who ensures that all children learn to read.

RESOURCES & FURTHER READING

14 Dyslexia TestsClinicians Like, http://dyslexiahelp.umich.edu/professionals/learn-about-dyslexia/diagnosing-dyslexia/tests/14-dyslexia-tests-clinicians-like

Dyslexia Laws 2019, https://www.dyslexicadvantage.org/dyslexia-laws-2018/

International Dyslexia Association, Dyslexia In the Classroom: What Every Teacher Needs to Know https://dyslexiaida.org/wp-content/uploads/2015/01/DITC-Handbook.pdf

Louise Spear-Swerling, PhD Here's Why Schools Should Use Structured Literacy, https://dyslexiaida.org/heres-why-schools-should-use-structured-literacy/

Scientific Evidence from the National Reading Panel www.lincs.ed.gov

Susan Barton, Warning Signs of Dyslexia: https://bartonreading.com/pdf/Dys-warning-signs1.pdf

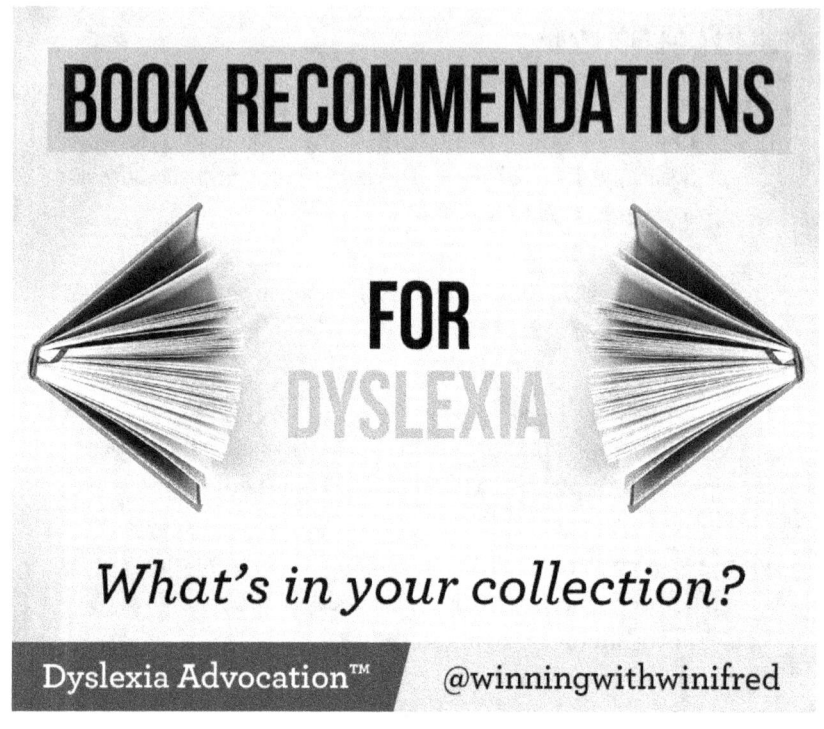

BOOK RECOMMENDATIONS

Overcoming Dyslexia by Sally Shaywitz, M.D.

The Dyslexic Advantage by Brock L. Eide, M.D., M.A., & Fernette F. Eide, M.D.

The Dyslexia Empowerment Plan by Ben Foss

Smart but Scattered by Peg Dawson, EdD, and Richard Guare, PhD

Winifred A. Winston

ABOUT THE AUTHOR

Winifred A. Winston is an enuthusiastic speaker, passionate advocate, bestselling author, and Founder & CEO of Dyslexia Advocation.™

After working as an administrator of a special education school and going through the IEP process in the public school system with her daughter, Winifred quickly realized African American parents lacked access to accurate information about dyslexia interventions and instructional strategies. With established industry contacts and a desire to help others, she founded Dyslexia Advocation ™ to equip parents with the tools to help their kids become successful readers.

Outside of work, Winifred is a volunteer state leader for Decoding Dyslexia Maryland and co-founder of their local advocacy and support group for parents and children in Baltimore City. She resides in Baltimore, MD with her daughter Logan where you can find them training for their next 5K.

COLLABORATIVE CO-TEACHING IN THE CLASSROOM

Jessica Reed, Ed.S.

Collaborative co-teaching can be confusing but can end up being the best thing in the classroom.

Imagine this:

You are a special education teacher and you have to work with a teacher, who everyone has said is a horrible co-teacher. You get nervous because you do not want to step on any toes in another person's classroom. You walk in and see the teacher, smiling and she says, "Hi!"

Or imagine you are a general education teacher, who has been told that you are going to have an inclusion teacher with you, whether you like it or not. You are frustrated because this is your classroom and your last few experiences have not gone well. So when the Special Education teacher walks into the room, you take a deep breath and smile and say "Hi!"

This type of situation is happening in classrooms all over the country because of the different needs of our students. Collaboration can be between general education teachers and special education teachers or general education teachers and paraprofessionals—basically, collaboration can happen in the classroom at any point.

Co-Teaching/collaboration is a tricky situation to be in the classroom for either the special education or general education teacher. Collaboration is very similar to being part of a marriage. At the beginning of the year, everything is rosy. By winter break, it could end up in divorce, or the marriage could be working and getting stronger every day.

There are many different ways to be able to improve this relationship and create a positive environment for everyone in the classroom.

There are many factors that can create or hinder the process of a positive collaboration between teachers in the classroom. These different factors include (but are not limited to) personal bias, teaching styles, values, how each person learns, and different backgrounds. Just like our students, each teacher comes to the classroom with a different story. This story may include personal experience from working with others to dealing with different family situations.

That's the beauty of collaboration, because two different-minded people get to spend time together and work together to make the learning environment a more fun and engaging space. Collaboration in the classroom can be a daunting but exciting task for all those who try to accomplish it during the school year.

Several different things need to happen to endure a positive experience, such as consistent planning, setting expectations, and sharing the workload for grading. Success may just depend on the different types of personalities that work together as the school year progresses.

What are some benefits of collaborating with a co-teacher? It gives the students an opportunity to learn from two separate teachers who may have their own personal strengths in certain areas. It also allows for the workload to be lightened in the classroom because you should be sharing responsibility.

Here are four different ways to make co-teaching a great process in the classroom:

1. Set up a rapport and work together: You do not have to like one another, but you need to be somewhat nice to each other. It is important to work together as a team so students do not sense a struggle between teachers to ensure learning is happening in the classroom.
2. Teaching Style (focus on strengths and weaknesses): Both teachers should identify your different teaching styles and how they look inr the classroom. It is crucial to figure out how you can complement each other.
3. IEPs/504/ESOL: We collaborate to ensure learning is equal for all students. Therefore it is vital to be able to communicate what all students need, especially when it is in an IEP (legal document).
4. Take Risks: Think outside of the box when it comes to lessons and activities! I have had the pleasure of working with the same co-teacher for the last two years. Her name is Mrs. Wright and she thinks completely out of the box. We have such a great time in her class and her students can tell that we really like each other. One of the out-of-the-box lessons that she does is having her students complete a murder mystery at our school after reading an Agatha Christie novel. All of the staff participates, and the students really enjoy the activity.

There are many different ways to ensure the collaboration is successful in the classroom and one way is to include Google and Google Classroom. So often, co-planning is not an option for teachers and Google can help with all of the various issues.

How can Google help in the collaborative classroom? Here are a few tools.

1. Google Calendar: Keep track of important events in the classroom.
2. Google Slides/Forms: Create presentations, forms, and even breakout sessions.
3. Google Docs can be used to keep anecdotal notes on students

and how the class is understanding an idea through the lessons.

Each teacher can have access to the students and can work with each group at different times, and Google Classroom can help with differentiation.

Using Google Classroom and sharing responsibilities for all students makes the load lighter for everyone and gives the kids more resources to use throughout the school day.

For collaboration to work in the classroom, communication is key. Everyone, including the teachers, will grow because of the positive impact that co-teaching has on learning.

Jessica Reed, Ed.S.

ABOUT THE AUTHOR

Jessica Reed is a special education teacher at a middle school in Georgia, who has been teaching for 11 years. Jessica's undergraduate degree is in Elementary Education from the University of Kentucky. She has a Masters of Arts in Collaborative Teaching (6-12) from the University of Alabama. Recently, Jessica graduated from Kennesaw State University with her Education Specialist in Instructional Technology. Jessica is a certified Google for Education Trainer and a Google Innovator (#NYC19). Jessica is married to Robby and they have one daughter, Elizabeth (2).

THE BEAUTY OF COLLABORATION

Aubrey Jones

A growing criticism of the American education system is that teachers spend too much of their time distanced from their colleagues. A recent survey found that teachers spend just 3% of their school day collaborating with other teachers. thus encouraging competition rather than collaboration. This makes it difficult for teachers to work together to solve educational and institutional issues. However, it doesn't have to be that way. There are many ways that teachers can reach out and connect with their colleagues and build a more collaborative atmosphere in their schools. The beauty of collaboration is not only the ability to tap into various perspectives and ideas, but also to share responsibility for our students' learning. The more that are invested in a student's education, the better the chance that student has to be successful.

It's been said that two minds are better than one, right? It's been proven that working together on a lesson plan can be a great way to get to know your colleagues and to build better lessons for your students. It should never feel like you are all alone or isolated from one another. Most importantly, you are able to share successes and failures with each other as you build relationships with your colleagues. When teachers come together to share information, resources, ideas, and expertise, learning becomes more accessible and effective for students (and lessons are more innovative). The best part about the benefits of teacher collaboration is that their ideas can be a reality—as they are are so many learning communities around the world and forums where they can exchange ideas. The focus of the collaboration is acknowledging, understanding, and working diligently to overcome the challenges and obstacles standing in the way of high-quality teacher collaboration (and share student successes!)

In addition, if you are seeing amazing results from students in your classroom, there is no reason not to share your techniques and lessons with other teachers. Teaching is all about sharing. It's possible that through collaboration, you can also draw on your colleagues' experiences with what works for them. In the end, the students' will benefit from the collaborated lessons. After all, it takes a village!

Even if your district does not allow joint collaboration, it is still possible to share your work and experiences through a collaborative blog. For example, I am really interested in bringing technology to students but my district did not have many resources. I was able to reach out to my professional learning network and have created a collaborative blog surrounding augmented reality experiences for my students. This has stretched me as an educator and held me accountable to implement new ideas. Above all I have connected with other educators. It is also a great way to talk when you don't have time at work, and it can be shared with other teachers outside your school as well.

We all know that there may not be time to discuss a collaborative movement during school. Creating an online forum or a chat room for teachers (even using Twitter) is a great way to share experiences, ideas, and ask for help at anytime. The beauty of collaboration is not only the ability to tap into various perspectives and ideas, but also to share responsibility for our students' learning. The more people invested in a student's education, the better the chance that student has to be successful. Technology plays a major role in modern teacher collaboration. Actively participating in a PLN on a social network gives you direct access to the knowledge, experience, and resources of countless educators who you may have never connected with in your immediate professional circles.

Twitter is an amazing digital hub for educators and educational resources. Create an account or log in to the one you haven't used since 2013 and follow educators you admire. Take it a step further by participating in relevant Twitter Chats—when a group of Twitter users (Tweeters?) meet at a predetermined time to discuss a particular topic.

Also, don't forget about the built-in capabilities that your district's learning management system (LMS) offers. You probably already have the tools to connect with colleagues and share ideas in an online community tailored to your district or school. It it has the communication and sharing tools you need, your LMS is the perfect place to create common assessments, track student data, share resources, and keep assignments.

It can be hard to hear a critique of your teaching or lessons, but, ultimately, it can be very helpful to you and other teachers to get some feedback. Think about it: How many other vocations allow people to come and observe? It is no easy task to let someone come and watch you teach. Teaching is personal, and being observed is nerve-wracking, often distracting to the students, and time-consuming for the teacher. Observation and networking with other educators helps us become more knowledgeable and productive. When we build a truly collaborative community of teachers from building to building and district to district, both teachers and students win. Some schools schedule observations or videotape teachers, but even informal feedback can be beneficial. I often say that "people learn more from what we do than what we say." I'm going to walk the walk and ask for feedback on my goals. I want to build on strengths and work on my weaknesses. I can only do this when I get rid of my blindspots.

Did I mention that it's scary? Did I also mention that I hope that the feedback I get is helpful and not hurtful? Don't teachers ask these same questions?

Asking others to come into your classroom and critique what you are doing is definitely daunting. But true growth can't happen in a vacuum.

Your peers and your leaders will admire you for trying to improve, and your students will understand that you care about them and their learning so greatly that you are willing to go out on a limb for them. So reflect on what aspects of teaching you want to become better at and post your #ObserveMe sign. Then put on your fearless hat and be ready for the amazing results of opening yourself and your classroom up!

One of the most common ways that teachers are battling feeling isolated from their peers is by building a personal learning network or community. This can be composed of teachers within your district or school or globally. . No matter who you choose to include, spend the time sharing, talking, and collaborating on educational projects and ideas so that your professional development grows along with it.There's absolutely no reason why educators have to solve a problem at your school or in your classroom all by yourself. Seek out other teachers for advice in helping find solid solutions to any sort of problem. Nothing fosters unity like working through something together.

Teaching can be a difficult profession which can, sometimes, make it easy to fall into habits of negativity. During my first year of teaching, understanding how to keep sane became a priority like never before. I learned that thinking positively led to acting out of my hope for a situation. If I projected an aura of trustful hope in a class and then backed it up with real instructional support, I saw real change. I'm still a young girl and I look even younger than I am (something I'm supposed to appreciate in the future). Having the experience of working with a lot of veteran teachers is both exciting and frustrating at times. Some want to handle you with kid gloves, telling you "everything is okay" and "you'll get it in time." While I appreciate the sentiment, the poor-little-puppy act offers no real concept of how to actively struggle as a teacher. Other teachers seem to dig their own chips into your shoulder and call it "advice."They want you to know how many hours until Friday, how many days until the next break, and how best to give in without being fired. It is as if the point of the job was to avoid discomfort while talking solely about how little comfort you're enjoying. Neither of these previous attitudes helps accomplish much of anything. The best veteran teachers can share stories of how to benefit from the worst situations and overcome through ownership.

Their relationship with everyone is visibly different than all others. The way those teachers speak with students mirrors how they act everywhere else. Their aim is to promote learning, reflection, and the hope for growth. That's the kind of teacher you want to become, the kind that inspired you to enter the field in the first place. **This is the kind of teacher and co-worker I want to be.**

Aubrey Jones

ABOUT THE AUTHOR

Aubrey is a special education teacher. She looks to eradicate labels in the classroom and in the community. She is on the forefront of a movement entitled #nomorelabels and is working to promote a classroom community of success with structure and support. When she does not have her teacher hat on, she creates comics and loves escaping to the beach. Fueled by caffeine she hopes to push kids beyond their comfort zone to try and experience new and exciting things. She will be opening a teacher's exchange (a place for teachers to connect, exchange resources and take care of themselves) in the near future. She is passionate about all kids succeeding and pushing beyond the status quo.

Twitter handle: spedteacheriam

Instagram: @justaubrey87

Podcast: Lessons and Lattes

Flipgrid: IEP101

https://justmeghansthought.blogspot.com/

LEVELING UP WITH DIGITAL BADGES

Adrienne Schlake, Dr. Jason Trumble, & Charlie Weber

Exploring the emergence of micro-credentialing and digital badging while analyzing the impact they can have on educators and students.

INTRODUCTION

We love to play video games. We love the challenge and strategy it takes to level up. In video games, digital badging is not a new concept. It is the thrill of the hunt, the effort for achievement, and the drive to prove oneself capable that engages the passion for gaming and the patience to learn from our own mistakes. When we earn a badge it tells me we've completed something unique and difficult. Whether it is a trophy on playstation, or an achievement in *World of Warcraft*, we get an adrenaline rush when we complete a difficult level or task. The badge becomes a symbol to myself and the rest of the community of my prowess.

I (Charlie) can vividly recall my first digital badge and the epic moment of earned recognition. I was the seventh person on a server of thousands to reach the new max level in *World of Warcraft: The Burning Crusa*d*e*. Earning that badge meant prestige and skill in my chosen gaming community. It drove me to continue earning the first boss kills, dungeon clears, and other in-game achievements that set me apart within the online gaming community.

Since this time of glory in the early 2000s, I have seen badges move from the world of gaming to the world of education and professional development. Education, as we know it, has changed. "Back in my day..." is the common phrase, and as everyone reading this can attest, the end of the sentence is a comparison to what it now is. K-12 classrooms are fully digital. Students are connected 1:1 with the newest iPads, Mac's or Chromebooks, and parents have access to grades 24/7. To say things have changed, and not analyze the way that learning has needed to shift in order to continue to effectively reach students and educators would be nefarious. In this chapter, the authors will define digital badging, share how badging crosses disciplines and industries, provide examples of how digital badges support teacher professional development, and explore the opportunities digital badging can have within the K-12 classroom and beyond.

DIGITAL BADGING

Digital badges are virtual stickers that represent an accomplishment or skill earned. These images come in many shapes, sizes, and colors. They are controlled by the issuing organization or institution.

Similar to online gaming, individuals can earn a variety of digital badges as they develop skills and competencies. As the popularity of badging has grown, a few questions that earners and providers must ask themselves are: What is the purpose of the badge? Are badges a form of mini-certification used to demonstrate formative knowledge, a representation of a one-time accomplishment, or an avatar to represent a passion? Do the badges truly *mean* anything?

Digital badging is more popular than ever and is growing in educational markets essentially gamifying professional development. Gamification of learning is a process of applying game design elements to a task (Lexico Online Dictionary, n.d.). Earning badges often includes elements of game design such as problem solving and task completion. There are many reasons for teachers to earn badges. They may have the goal of helping one's learning community. They may have a mandate to grow and develop a particular skill. They may simply be seeing a tiny acknowledgment of something that distinguishes them as unique in the world of education. The gamification of the process helps learners through challenges and prolonged engagement in learning as they earn their badge.

Gamification of learning through digital badging is one way to help promote the growth mindset that educators model for learners. As teachers earn their first badge, they can often continue their learning and professional growth by completing more advanced modules that indicate more expertise, skill, and knowledge. This continual growth model allows teachers to continually learn and document that learning through digital badges. That teacher who has the desire to continually develop can find recognition in the badges they earn.

Badges are also a way to help answer common questions that arise in education like: *"Are you good with Google?"* Well, how does one quantify that? Is the question referring to email, calendar, sheets, docs, presentations, or sites? The vastness of Google makes it difficult to respond without follow-up questions, but in digital professional (development) circles, a badge that shows the individual *is* knowledgeable in a certain area, and provides instant credibility. The individual becomes a valuable resource to the educational community and can be seen as a leader in that specific area.

Badges have become a disruptive force in the industry according to David Leaser, Senior Program Executive, Innovation and Growth Initiatives at IBM, and Founder of the IBM Digital Badge Program. "In just a few short years, Open Badges have barnstormed into the accreditation space, providing a unique way to issue a credential which can be shared instantly on social sites – the perfect marriage between social media and credentials/recognition. Badges can be issued for a wide variety of activities, like course completions or proof of a real skill or competence" (Leaser, 2019).

Certifications and Open Badges: Complements in a T Skills Model

CERTIFICATIONS				
Legally defensible / psychometrically sound	Shelf life of 24 months or more	Required by an industry governing body	Required for safety or security	Is required by state law or license

BADGES
Liquid skills that change quickly
Continuing education credits
Passions and interests
Demonstrated capabilities
Inventions and innovations

Open badges are digital badges that include metadata and are shareable across digital platforms. Any company or institution can create an open badge to validate a badge earner allowing their successes to be widely shared.

There are a myriad of badges that an educator can earn and most are promoted by companies who want teachers to use their products. Apple has the Apple Teacher badge which can be earned by completing online modules that introduce teachers to Apple software and hardware in the context of teaching. Apple also offers modules for introductions to teaching coding. Google has offered its Educator Certification for a few years now. Interested educators can participate in an estimated 13 hours of online tutorials then pay a small fee to take a test for Level One certification. They also offer a Level Two certification as well as Google Trainer status.

The International Society for Technology in Education (ISTE) recently created a program where teachers can earn their certification and badge. The teacher must participate in a two-day in-person professional development workshop and then complete an online course as they develop a portfolio. Upon approval, the participants become ISTE Certified Educators and they get a digital badge. Currently, the ISTE Certification is the only non-device or non-software specific badging opportunity for educators to show competency in a range of standards. Most badges are supported by companies and are connected to specific digital technologies. Badging is becoming mainstream with educators, and these certifications, like being Google Certified or ISTE certified, are making their way into email signatures, and social media biography sections.

MOTIVATION

Passion. Curiosity. Intrinsic. Extrinsic. How are you motivated? How do you motivate others? In the realm of education, specifically teaching, students are motivated in many, many different ways. Any classroom teacher would attest to students who were intrinsically motivated. These lucky souls sought success because they had an internal drive toward academic excellence and achievement. Completion, As, playing in the big basketball game, whatever it was, it was internal.

On the other side are those students who are extrinsically motivated. These are the students that don't work with Plan A. Plan B is generally not "it" either. These are the students that teachers *work* for. That the teachers help to find, bait, then show how to bite the hook. These students are the lucky ones that teachers *get to* seek out ways to engage in different learning styles. They are the ones who teachers write curriculum specifically for, and then rewrite for success. For positive behavior. For building study habits. For becoming life-long, passionate, curious learners.

Through the evolution of schools—classrooms, teachers, students, technology, etc., changes are constant. There are, however, some roots that have been planted so deeply that the path to achievement may change, yet the finish line is still the same. What gets all of us there is motivation, intrinsic and extrinsic.

Intrinsic Motivation Theory refers to behavior that is driven by internal rewards. In other words, the motivation to engage in a behavior arises from within the individual because it is naturally satisfying to you. There have been a number of different proposed theories to explain intrinsic motivation and how it works. Some experts believe that all behavior is driven by external reward, such as money, status, or food. In intrinsically motivated behaviors, the reward is the activity itself. ("Intrinsic Motivation Theory: Overview, Factors, and Examples", 2019)

Motivation is vitally important for effective learning. Using badges to increase prolonged motivation can support students learning. Another lens to view intrinsic and extrinsic motivation is by the Greek philosopher Aristotle. He separated motives into two ends and means. Ends are indicated when a person engages in behavior for no apparent reason other than that is what the person **desires** to do. Contrast that with a mean when the person action is directed by a different result, the mean leads to an end. A student who reads ahead in a book because of the love for reading is exhibiting what we would label intrinsic motivation or Aristotle's end. Compare that to a student who reads ahead in the book because they want to do well on the quiz at the end of the book. The second student is exhibiting extrinsic motivation or Aristotle's mean, it is not the book or reading the student is after, but a good grade.

Having a passion to find oneself standing in front of a group of students day-in and day-out, teaching, motivating, explaining, reteaching, creating, and failing, is not for the faint-of-heart. These individuals, teachers, as a group, are life-long learners. They are, as a profession, naturally, growth-oriented, possess a growth-mindset, and are curious. Teachers want to be good. They don't pursue the profession of education to fail. They understand that failure is a part of growth, and choose to grow. This idea, coupled with the ever-changing technology, has allowed teachers the opportunity to seek professional learning networks far outside of what a school and district offer.

COMPETENCY-BASED LEARNING

Online access to professional learning networks and Digital Badging have exploded and are marketed toward educators. Back-in-the-day, teachers used to earn their diploma, pay for their state certification, and enter a classroom with that being the only "badge" they needed. They purchased their dresses and ties, were handed the book with the answers in it, and they took off on a grand adventure. Thank goodness for all of us that times have changed.

Continuing to throw back to the evolution of educators, the influx of advanced degree-holding and nationally-certified teachers was a distinguishing factor in the circle of education. It meant that teachers were, on their own, going beyond the minimum requirements. Teachers wanted more knowledge. More skills. More pedagogy.

Teachers, with their curiosity and passion, are thriving. In droves, they are becoming believers of professional learning networks, online/content-specific webinars, and mini-courses. Teachers believe in the power of unlimited resources, and are looking for new ways to implement old ideas. The technology-driven generation of students are here, and with that, teachers are on-board with helping aim students and their motivation.

Now, teachers want more for their students. Teachers want instant. Teachers want their students to have applicable, beneficial, and demonstrable skills and understanding. Enter the idea of microcredentialing within individual, personal, professional development, and cross that over for students. Digital badging, the process of earning the proverbial 21st-century "gold star sticker" demonstrates completion of a course, participation within an event, demonstration of knowledge or skills, and many other things.

ONWARD

With all the badges available, what do they do for teachers? Within a classroom, do badges offer more validation to your students? Do they care about how many you have? That you're the "groundbreaker" or that you've "attended a conference"? No. From experience, students do not. They actually just look at you funny. But, what the badges mean as far as from a personal and professional standpoint, is that they are important in an educator's own professional learning network development.

In an ever more increasing online world of professional learning network (PLN) development, badges are an important delineator of microcredentials that distinguish participants, and individualize participants' learning. They help to create subsections of like-trained individuals who can contribute to the collective, professional growth.

Teachers with a growth mindset are almost always involved in many different PLNs that are outside of the building and district-sponsored norm. They connect to other educators through active Facebook groups, subject or content-specific state and national organizations, Twitter chats, and even degree programs. In order to create a sense of accomplishments among growth mindset teachers, badges are a way to share accomplishments and completions of trainings. Badges validate the participants' expertise and can support the co-construction of knowledge within a group.

According to Odelia Younge, senior project director for educator micro-credentials at Digital Promise, in the ESchoolNews article "How Educator Micro-Credentials Support Professional Learning," badges have four main design traits: Competency-based, On-demand, Shareable, and Personalized ("How educator micro-credentials support PL", 2019). All four traits work together to increase the value and impact on educators and their professional learning networks, as well as the students with whom they connect.

As you consider badges in the classroom, let us wonder together on some possibilities. Could the badge be used to highlight a student's accomplishments, instead of their deficiencies? As an example, if students are working on their math factors, 1-12, a student who is struggling can be celebrated for their growth at each step. Little victories to help encourage the student and let them track their progress. Day 1) The student did factors 1-4, Day 3) Factors 5, 9, 12, Day 6) 6, Day 9) 7, 8, 11. This becomes a tool of encouragement to let the child see their progress, and you as an educator to cheer the child on for their grit. Can badges be used to help with inequality, socio-economic, racial, language, learning styles or skills? Badges do not need to be a permanent fixture attached to the student. Instead, the badge could be for behaviors you want to cultivate in your classroom, or for classroom jobs.

Ultimately, the emergence of micro-credentialing and digital badging has a direct impact on educators and students. Education, as we know it, has changed. Through this chapter, examining the badging that crosses disciplines and industries, and identifying how digital badges support teacher professional development, the opportunities that digital badging can have within the K-12 classroom and beyond is exponential. This is the future of distinguishing and individualizing professional development.

REFERENCES

Gamification (n.d.) In *Lexico Online Dictionary*. Retrieved September 20, 2019 from https://www.lexico.com/en/definition/gamification

How educator micro-credentials support PL. (2019). Retrieved 30 August 2019, from https://www.eschoolnews.com/2019/07/30/how-educator-micro-credentials-support-pl/

Intrinsic Motivation Theory: Overview, Factors, and Examples. (2019). Retrieved 31 August 2019, from https://www.healthline.com/health/intrinsic-motivation#how-it-works

Leaser, D. (2019). Open Badges vs. Certifications: Is there a battle brewing in the IT credential market? - IBM Training and Skills Blog. Retrieved 30 August 2019, from https://www.ibm.com/blogs/ibm-training/open-badges-vs-certifications-is-there-a-battle-brewing-in-the-it-credential-market/

PHOTO CITATION

Leaser, D. (2019). Open Badges vs. Certifications: Is there a battle brewing in the IT credential market? - IBM Training and Skills Blog. Retrieved 30 August 2019, from https://www.ibm.com/blogs/ibm-training/open-badges-vs-certifications-is-there-a-battle-brewing-in-the-it-credential-market/

ABOUT THE AUTHORS

Adrienne Schlake

Adrienne Schlake is a certified Spanish Teacher, Head Golf Coach, and Assistant Mountain Biking Coach at The New School in Fayetteville. She is the 2018 recipient of the ARKSTE Making IT Happen award, and is currently working on a K-12 School Administration Endorsement at the University of Arkansas. She holds a masters degree in curriculum and instruction from the University of Nebraska, and is the President-Elect of ARKSTE, the Arkansas state affiliate of ISTE. Her years of classroom experience range in Spanish and ELL, from public to private schools in Nebraska and Arkansas, and piloting a variety of technology with her districts as they integrate 1:1. Adrienne also serves on the board for the Arkansas Foreign Language Teachers Association, and proudly shares a classroom with her licensed school Therapy Dog, Luna.

Dr. Jason Trumble

Dr. Jason Trumble is an Assistant Professor of Education at the University of Central Arkansas. He is an ISTE Certified Educator and holds multiple educational technology certifications. Dr. Trumble teaches a variety of courses for preservice and in-service teachers, and engages teachers in meaningful professional development. Dr. Trumble has a wide-ranging research agenda including how to improve teachers' understanding of content, pedagogy, and technology, as well as investigating makerspaces and maker pedagogies. Dr. Trumble is in his 16th year as a professional educator with experience in California, Texas, and Arkansas.

Charles Weber

Charles Weber is a professional problem solver. He trained as a marriage and family therapist, graduating with a Masters in Counseling from John Brown University. He currently works in public schools as a member of the IT department. He was ARKSTE president from 2017-2020, and involved with the local technology non-profit NWA Tech-Fest as a board member. His goal is to free educators from the burden of technology, while empowering technology to personalize learning.

GAMING BUSINESS EDUCATION - LET'S PLAY!

Kathleen H. Fuller, M.S.Ed.

Play, entrepreneurship, and management are concepts in business. Risk-taking, changing habits, and cognitive and creative rigor stem from these big three.

Playing games and creating games not only can teach high-level concepts but also build collaborative learning skills. Creating games develops rigorous learning connections to entrepreneurship, innovation, and the iterative cycles of business development.

The instructional pedagogy of gaming and game creation used in my HS business classroom are compatible in any classroom.

The news is filled with headlines of teacher strikes, underperforming schools, and conflicting curriculum goals. Yet every day, countless teachers are making magic in their classrooms, from urban to rural, affluent to impoverished; these teachers, some with little to no knowledge of business process analysis, are doing just that! They analyze, they incentivize, they deal with human resources issues and motivation and continue to be productive.

Play - Entrepreneurship - Management; three words that most people would not put together when speaking about education; however, in my tenure as an entrepreneur coach, instructional developer, adjunct professor, athlete and coach, singer and performer, and teacher of Business and Career Education and Social Studies with over 30 years in the classroom, meeting rooms and server rooms throughout New York State and Western Massachusetts, I have worked to empower my students and clients by teaching innovation, iteration and integration through project and problem-based learning and gaming and I have seen its results firsthand!

Not only are these three words, Play - Entrepreneurship - Management connected, but optimal in students' deep understanding of the oftentimes difficult and unfamiliar vocabulary of vocational or any of their studies.

We are inherently problem-solvers by nature. We are curious and crave connections. We love to play.

Gaming is the ideal platform to make learning "stick"—to afford students deeper leveling, broader reaching, and easier recalling of curricular concepts.

Like gum under a desk, students use games, play, and the iterative methodologies to not only form good learning habits, but also to transform into becoming managers of their own learning, entrepreneurs of their ideas and players of a self-determined future—the sticky learning concepts we all epitomize.

So why don't we play more?

In my classroom we do! I started my year off with an ice-breaker activity, by asking my students to name their three (3) favorite games.

Surprisingly, it became a question fraught with more questions. Some were:

"Can I write down a video game?"

"Do you want me to name a board game?"

"How about a puzzle?"

"Are playing sports a game?"

"What about the playground games like Four Square, is that a game?"

Amazed by what I thought was a simple question that would take no more than three minutes, a simple ice breaker, this one question turned into a complex cognitive activity.

My students overcomplicated it, so I turned their questions into more questions by asking them, "What do YOU think?"

I told them I was was not limiting them. I told them to just simply write down the first three games that came to their minds that they enjoyed.

Why were they so afraid to go with their gut answer? Why were they so afraid to just write it down?

In other words, why were my students conditioned to feel as if even the simplest of questions had a right or wrong answer?

Why were they afraid to fail? Why were they afraid to fail at something that was unfailable?

Or was I the failure because my question was poorly-written?

What is it? What is so ingrained, so cellular, that we can't envision the simplest of mistakes?

Do we like failure? The simple answer, NO!

My question then is why not?

It hurts.

This is where cognitive theory kicks in. In discussing gaming and learning with my "crew" (A group formed from the onset of the Games in Education Symposium[1] in the Capital District of NYS that encompasses teachers, game developers business people) and oftentimes we speak of the challenges of the neurotypical mindset as non-neurotypical learners. We also wonder if non-neurotypical is a better way to create challenging material.

What can we learn from non-neurotypical learners? Are all learners non-neurotypical but conditioned to be neurotypical through habit? How can we break the habits to form better neurological connections?

Malcolm Gladwell calls them "Outliers," business teachers call them innovators (entrepreneurs), cognitive scientists call them non-neurotypical, and historians call them rebels.

Perhaps more simply put, ~~some,~~ no, many people enjoy coloring outside the lines in a world full of boxes drawn in permanent marker.

We speed just a little bit. We put just enough coins in a parking meter and try to stretch out a minute or two more. We show up at 7:20 am for a 7:30 am appointment...

So if most people want to take risks, why don't we call it that? Why don't we fess up to wanting to make mistakes and own them when we make them?

Why are schools encountering more and more students that are non-neurotypical or on the autism spectrum?

According to the Autism Society: "Prevalence of autism in U.S. children increased by 119.4 percent from 2000 (1 in 150) to 2010 (1 in 68). (CDC, 2014)[2] Autism is the fastest-growing developmental disability... and its prevalence has increased by 6-15 percent each year from 2002 to 2010."

How do we, as teachers encountering more and more students that are non-neurotypical, (Note: Non-neurotypical learners are students most commonly placed on the autism spectrum but this term can be used with any student that does not benefit from or has difficulty with learning in traditional ways.) address the learning needs of the increasing number of students presenting with these learning types while allowing those who enjoy the structure of neurotypical lessons and procedures through either preference or as I dare say "habits," create engaging and robust lessons?

Well, by incorporating gaming of course!

When in the 1950's Professor Leon Festinger's in his groundbreaking book, <u>Theory of Cognitive Dissonance</u> stated, "when there were discrepancies of opinion or ability among the members of a group, pressures arose to reduce such discrepancies." He also wrote:

1. Dissonance results when an individual must choose between attitudes and behaviors that are contradictory.
2. Dissonance can be eliminated by reducing the importance of the conflicting beliefs, acquiring new beliefs that change the balance, or removing the conflicting attitude or behavior.

We feel the pain. We don't like it. So we do everything in our power not to feel it. We push away anything that is different to "fit in" or to just make the pain go away. We habitualize our experience to create habits.

We may not like doing things the way everyone else does them, but we crave acceptance and hate the pain so we have engaged in learning methods that may not be the best for us.

We then take that learned experience about risk avoidance from schools into the workplace. We fear taking risks because we fear condemnation, losing jobs and/or status. It can create toxic work cultures. As an organizational management consultant, I have been involved in workplace improvement projects that take a year or more due to the resistance to change cellularly ingrained in our being.

If we want to create the employees and entrepreneurs of the future, how does this cognitive dissonance thwart discovery, inquiry, and change in the educational setting?

How do we go from the scientific, exploratory and risk-taking toddlers to the fear-filled, settlers of the status quo?

How does this subversion of creativity and discovery learning from our childhood continue onto the workplace? How do we, in turn, address this shameful statistic that "35 percent of young adults (ages 19-23) with autism have not had a job or received postgraduate education after leaving high school" (Shattuck et al., 2012)?

To me, students are just employees and entrepreneurs in training. Their ideas, suggestions and prior learning MUST be valued, acknowledged and, painfully at times, corrected if we are to create the social change agents and entrepreneurs of the future.

We must teach them about cognitive dissonance and about the pain that comes with failure without stifling the growth and creation that can spring from it. (Festinger)

We are told, by administrators, the public, and the media that as teachers, we should create a learning environment that creates a safe and productive learning place for all of our students.

So how do we accomplish that with the oftentimes limited financial resources, oversized classrooms and over-taxed time schedules of teachers, students, and families?

My answer came by developing a business process analysis model for educational purposes through gaming after asking myself the question, "How can I pull my unique knowledge of organizational management, employee motivation, and the habitual nature of what makes worksplaces successful and games fun and use it to make my students' 'user experiences' better?"

Businesses of learning—make no mistake, school is business. Not-for-profits are still businesses and therefore need to be viewed through a business mindset. How can we as teachers utilize the boundless studies on workplace performance to assist us in helping our students be better learners? We want them to enjoy learning, to crave more of it, not see it as an enemy. We want to produce a service (education) that more and more customers crave and create a positive experience when engaging in it.

We as teachers need to take risks, and to allow our students to do the same in a safe environment to change the oftentimes bad habits of education.

In other words, we need to PLAY GAMES!

So I hit the books. I dug out my undergraduate business textbooks and articles. I researched successful business leaders and the brain based learning theories that they engaged in to change bad habits and improve their users' (employees') experiences. I talked to my friends and colleagues.

Paul O'Neill in October of 1987 as the new CEO of Alcoa decided to make a small but substantive change in the way Alcoa did business. He decided to focus on worker safety. That was relatively unheard of in those days of fierce Japanese competition within the metals manufacturing industry. That one "small" change led to a quintupling of Alcoa's profits.

In a nutshell, Mr O'Neill changed habits.

Schools, and by extension, teachers, are like airplanes. Oftentimes there are problems with the inner workings that cause the oxygen masks to fall from the ceiling.

Discipline problems, unsafe home lives of our students, substance abuse, truancy, cheating, absenteeism, tardiness, disruptive behaviors—all of these are things that individually can send a plane down and when multiplied, can bring the plane and our oxygen masks from the ceilings.

Our first reaction is to put the oxygen mask on our students. But as everyone knows from the demonstrations on the airplanes putting YOUR oxygen mask on first, allows you to have the strength to give O_2 to help those around you.

But how?

Focusing on righting the airplane by focusing on teachers FIRST.

"It should go without saying, if the person who works at your company is 100 percent proud of the brand and you give them the tools to do a good job and they are treated well, they're going to be happy," Richard Branson tells *Inc.* president and editor-in-chief Eric Schurenberg."If the person who works at your company is not appreciated, they are not going to do things with a smile," Branson says.

How do you get that smile? How do you get teachers to feel as if they matter and that they are valued?

In out professional meetings we need to play games. We as teachers need to learn more about how playing games affects learning and we need to listen to business learners and entrepreneurs, watch TED Talks and continue to learn about how game theory can improve user experiences.

Ok, I know, I know…it seems crazy, but I have questions about when you play games in your classroom be it online, teacher directed "Kahoot" or "Jeopardy" type, or just letting your students play a card game like "Uno" during free time or recess.

What do your students look like? Are they smiling? Do they push through frustrations after losing a game and try again? Are you smiling and happy?

Isn't this what we want our students to do in their learning? Isn't this what YOU want to be doing?

Let us take it one step further now. Imagine having the student, who may not be engaged in the lesson, but who you observe drawing beautiful pictures. They obviously enjoy that and have a talent. Why not engage that talent into creating a game with a team of others in the class?

Why not have them take the learning objectives and concepts of the content and create a game?

Let your students naturally figure out who is good at what, figure out what game modality would best address the content, create a materials list, storyboard the game play, collaborate to find the answers, and present that to other students by developing the rules for their game along with the finished product.

They can briefly explain their game in a roundtable or direct presentation style to the others in the class and let the other students do an analysis of their playing experiences with tips to the creators as to how to make it better and thereby engage in a peer analysis.

Then take it a step further—ask other teachers and/or parents/members of the community to sit on a panel of investors and have these student creators pitch their game to them.

Cognitively robust, collaborative, and creative are the three phrases that come to mind in that educational exercise as well as play, entrepreneurship, and management.

Through play, gaming, and game development, students engage in entrepreneurial, collaborative, and creative processes and learn self-and team-management techniques.

Through learning through play and game-creation they hit upon every Level 4 in Danielson's *Framework For Teaching*.

So take a risk, play "Risk," encourage risks in your classroom. Gaming is a great tool to change habits, improve learning outcomes, and prepare students for the future workplace.

REFERENCES

Baer, D. (2014, April 9). How Changing One Habit Helped Quintuple Alcoa's Income. Retrieved from https://www.businessinsider.com/how-changing-one-habit-quintupled-alcoas-income-2014-4

Danielson, C. (2013). The Framework for Teaching Evaluation Instrument. Retrieved from https://usny.nysed.gov/rttt/teachers-leaders/practicerubrics/Docs/danielson-teacher-rubric.pdf

Duhigg, C. (2014). *The power of habit: why we do what we do in life and business*. New York: Random House Trade Paperbacks.

(2015, August 26). Facts and Statistics. Retrieved from https://www.autism-society.org/what-is/facts-and-statistics/

(n.d.). Games in Education Symposium. Retrieved from http://gamesineducation.org/

Gladwell, M. (2008). *Outliers*. New York, NY: Little, Brown and Company.

Oppong, T. (2018, June 15). The Neuroscience of Change: How to Train Your Brain to Create Better Habits. Retrieved from https://medium.com/swlh/to-break-bad-habits-you-really-have-to-change-your-brain-the-neuroscience-of-change-da735de9afdf

Raymundo, O. (2014, October 28). Richard Branson: Companies Should Put Employees First. Retrieved from https://www.inc.com/oscar-raymundo/richard-branson-companies-should-put-employees-first.html

Roth, M. (2012, May 13). 'Habitual excellence': The workplace according to Paul O'Neill. Retrieved from https://www.post-gazette.com/business/businessnews/2012/05/13/Habitual-excellence-The-workplace-according-to-Paul-O-Neill/stories/201205130249

Kathleen H. Fuller, M.S. Ed.

ABOUT THE AUTHOR

Kathleeen H. Fuller, M.S. Ed. - a first generation college graduate, and an unlikely educator, trained in statistical economics and history, Kathy came to teaching at the behest and compliments of her undergraduate college professors and has never looked back.

For over three decades Kathy has worked as an entrepreneur coach, IT professional, instructional developer, adjunct professor, technical editor, fundraising and development professional, coach, singer, performer and teacher of Business and Career Education and Social Studies in the classroom, meeting, server and board rooms or wherever she was needed throughout New York State and Western Massachusetts,. Kathy has worked to empower her students and clients by teaching innovation, iteration and integration through project and problem based learning and gaming.

She lives in the Tech Valley of NYS with her husband and has three adult and two teenage offspring. They have and continue at times to be her test subjects, game theorists and teachers and are her happiest and proudest accomplishments.

PART TWO: IDENTITY

ADDING TO THE SINGLE STORY

Jason Trinh

Finding your voice to share your story to add to the greater collective.

On any given weekend, you probably find me and my daughters at the public library, getting our weekly haul of picture books starring Anna or Elsa. As I look through the stacks, I can't help but be drawn to the books where characters look like me: straight black hair with narrow brown eyes and light-brown skin tone. There are two types of books I see where there are Asian characters. One type are cultural books celebrating the Mid-Autumn Festival or stories sharing the traditions of the Lunar New Year. The other type is a limited or non-speaking role where the lead has an Asian friend or classmate. This is the single story that I grew up with and now my kids are growing up with. This story isn't limited to the Asian and Pacific-Islander community, but to all people of colour where the stories we read as kids, the stories we read our own kids and the stories we read our students omit racialized characters or are added with no intention or depth. The same realization occurred with another father named Jerry Zhang where his oldest daughter told him that she didn't want to be Chinese anymore as none of the characters looked like her. Jerry decided to create his own book series with a female protagonist that happens to be Asian. On his Kickstarter page he writes, 'while it's important for children to learn about their cultures through books, it's equally important for Asian children to see themselves represented in books as interesting and smart individuals rather than just products of their cultures." There is power in seeing yourself in different spaces. As an educator in the edtech space, I am struck with the same feelings of looking through the stacks of the library where I am looking for faces that look like mine.

I entered the edtech space like many where my gateway drug was Twitter. My eyes were opened to the amazing things that other educators were doing and different events that were happening! I attended my first edtech Summit and I realized that I had found my people and I got a serious case of the edtech fever with the symptoms of presenting workshops and getting certifications. One of the treatment to my edtech fever was the Google for Education Certified Innovator Academy, where I was humbled to be part of the Washington DC cohort in 2017. As I dove deeper into the edtech space, I noticed that there were a limited number of educators of colour that lead workshops and even fewer found on the keynote stages. At the 2018 ISTE conference, I was amazed and changed by Patricia Brown's address where she shared her story of being an educator after tragedy struck her community. In this address, I saw an educator of colour on the big stage passionately sharing her story and was impacted by it as I saw what was possible. Did I have a story to tell? Could I be part of the solution to diversify the edtech space? Do I have the courage to share?

The answers to these questions came in attending the Our Voice Academy. Created and lead by Jennie Magiera (Founder and President of Our Voice Alliance), this academy brought together a group of educators of color to learn how to craft and deliver a keynote address. Before I attended the Our Voice Academy, I had a single story of what it was. I knew I was going to meet other educators of color and start crafting an address, but I soon discovered something deeper.

As powerfully described in Chimamanda Ngozi Adichie's talk, *The Danger of a Single Story*, I had only one perception of what this was from seeing tweets (#OVAcademy) and reading blog posts because it cannot be described in words. Like trying to draw a three-dimensional object on a piece of blank white paper, you may capture pieces of it, but not everything. To really capture what is Our Voice Academy, you need to feel the emotion in the room, you need to see eye to eye and connect with another person, you need to hear the music and the stories, you need to speak your truth and you need to smell all of us breaking bread together and building community - This is the perfect experience.

The coaches (Jennie Magiera, Dee Lanier, Monica I. Martinez, and Sarah Thomas) all provided so much of themselves to help us grow and I am thankful and humbled to have spent time with them and learned from them. I learned the importance of being intentional with your voice and body. When telling a story, it is so much more than the words you are saying, it is how you say it and how motion can enhance it. I learned that the feelings of nervousness can be channelled as excitement. I learned the true sense of the saying that "a picture is worth a thousand words", where images and design can tell their own stories. Finally, I learned that we can improve our storytelling skills until they become natural or an unconscious competence.

Our Voice Academy help me find my voice and my confidence is growing and I see that my stories as being valuable. I have a family that is here to celebrate the successes, provide support during the challenges and to be critically kind in feedback. Many educators, like you, may feel that your stories are ordinary or not impactful, but those stories that you feel are common are what make them relatable and your reflection on them makes them unique. I was inspired by the courage and vulnerability of my cohort to share their stories and I want to empower you to share your story on stages (big or small) that you have access to. The best way to get a sense of Our Voice Academy is to be courageous and share your story in the next tweet, blog post or summit stage. After sharing your story, gravitate toward those that reach out, those who see you, hear you and feel you. These are the people that will help amplify your voice.

We all have a story to tell and the more narratives we see and hear on the big stages, we add to the single story of different races, genders, sexual orientations, religions, abilities or ages. We need to be courageous to share our stories and just like the Cowardly Lion from the Wizard of Oz, when you surround yourself with a supportive community you will be able to find the courage (that you always had) to act.

Jason Trinh

ABOUT THE AUTHOR

Jason Trinh (@jasontries) is a Hybrid-Teacher-Coach in the Toronto District School Board. Jason is a Google Innovator and Apple Distinguished Educator, who actively shares his passion for educational technology as a speaker and facilitator at conferences throughout North

America. Jason is passionate about STEM education utilizing the inquiry/design process to find solutions to authentic problems as well as making STEM education accessible as a Toronto Science Fair Coordinator. He is the founder of the Racialized Educators for Action & Leadership (RacializedEDU.com) and member of Our Voice Academy, working for greater diversity, equity and inclusion in all educational spaces and empowering all voices to tell their story. He is the winner of the Premier's Award for Teaching Excellence and the ISTE Digital Equity PLN Award.

RACE MATTERS FOR THIS WHITE TEACHER

Melody McAllister

In 2004, I began my first year of teaching. I lived in a small Texas town and the population of students I served was almost 99.9% White. However, after marrying my husband, my fourth year of teaching began while helping start up a new school in an area outside of Dallas. The neighborhood around it was full of large, beautiful homes, but the children living in those homes would not be the students coming through our doors. We bussed in more than 70% of our students, and our student body was mostly Hispanic and African Americans. Each year, our student body grew. Sometimes we were the largest elementary in our district, but our largest two populations were always Hispanic and African American. Our Muslim and Asian populations grew each year, too. For every year that I taught at this school, I only had a few White students, yet we still had a staff who was mostly White.

Before this new elementary school opened, I was definitely nervous about teaching at a diverse campus. I wondered if I would be able to reach my students, and if this new community I was living and teaching in would accept me? It's no surprise that I had some awkward run-ins with parents that first year. The majority of parents spoke Spanish, and apparently I looked like the White stepmother of one of my Black, female students. Her mother did not like that at all. After the mother told me this at a parent conference, she also wanted to know if her daughter "acted White?" Growing up, we did not talk about color as it was considered impolite, so these frank conversations with parents challenged my thinking processes. Even so, it wasn't hard for me to bond with my Students Of Color, but I was learning from them how to respond and address our differences.

Looking back on these situations, I know I could have handled them better if I was the person I am today. But those first years at our new school helped me see that race issues do exist. Bonds with my students were definitely developed and strong- but with the things I know now- I would love to go back in time and give those kids an even better fifth grade experience. Over the next few years, my Students Of Color and their parents would support, challenge, and teach me how to be a better educator.

COMING TO TERMS WITH MY OWN PREJUDICE

I'm a White woman teaching in a school and district whose student population is not reflected in our teacher population. Like many schools across our nation, this is a problem. I didn't know it was a problem until one of my Black colleagues explained this to me. The conversation we had was very eye-opening and made me aware of why students need people in their lives to be representative of who they could find connections & commonalities. It wasn't that I should quit because I am White, but acknowledging this as a relevant issue is important to help me connect with all the people in my community: students, parents, *and teachers*, too!! It's not a secret we are losing good teachers every year because they don't have the necessary support, but it's even more prevalent in our African American teachers. We need them in our school communities, but their numbers are growing smaller.

Microaggressions are:

brief and commonplace daily verbal, behavioral, and environmental indignities, whether intentional or unintentional, that communicate hostile, derogatory, or negative racial slights and insults that potentially have harmful or unpleasant psychological impact on the target person or group.

— (SOLORZANO, CEJA, & YOSSO, 2000 IN UNIVERSITY OF DENVER, N.D.)

After learning more from my Friends of Color, the first thing I started doing was reflecting on my own microaggressions. A teacher may assume a Black student will be a discipline problem before knowing her, and when discipline is needed, giving that student a harsher punishment. When I became more aware of my own, I did think about how I handled discipline issues and asked myself if I was being tougher on my Black students. I would run things by my Colleagues Of Color to get a better idea when I wasn't sure if I was making the best decision for a child. I talked more to parents, asked them how I could support them at school in a way that was reflective of what was working at home. The longer I taught, the more I welcomed parents in my classroom, and asked for their feedback before making a disciplinary move. When we had parent teacher meetings, I never felt like we were on opposing sides as we were there to help a child that both of us loved and this created a supportive environment. I believe knowing our own prejudices will help guide us in honest reflection and allow room in our minds and souls to replace falsehoods with truth.

But make no mistake, coming to terms with one's own prejudice is not easy or something to be flippant about. Often we can't even see it without others pointing it out. We can be defensive and make excuses, or we can take action and examine our thought patterns to train our minds to go beyond our first thoughts. Prior to frank conversations with my colleagues and rethinking my own patterns, my thoughts. could be summed up like this:

First of all, I did not believe I was prejudiced against Brown or Black people. I believed I was color blind, that we were all the same, and in this modern time we were all offered the same opportunities. I believed the only thing that separated us was that some of us chose to take on opportunities while others did not. White privilege could not exist because we have laws in place for that. I was not to blame for any societal racism as I did not own slaves nor even exist before or during The Civil Rights Movement—which seemed to me a long-ago history. The Black Lives Matter movement made no sense to me! All lives matter and to say anything else was, in fact, racist. If these Black people would just listen to the orders given by the police, we'd stop seeing these shootings and riots on the news every week!

Coming to terms with this thinking has helped me develop more genuine relationships with parents and students. It has led to my own reflection on how I may discipline Students Of Color differently than others.

THERE ARE THREE MAIN REASONS I'VE CHANGED:

1. Ongoing conversations with my Black friends, whom I completely respect. My friends Natalie and Derek especially come to my mind as they were so patient with me. I listened to their stories and perspectives. On social media and face to face, I have sought out those willing to have an honest conversation about race. I have always grown afterwards and thank all of my friends who do not shrink back from these conversations. But the most important thing to remember during these conversations is to acknowledge the truth the Person Of Color is sharing. Many times we look at our life experiences differently. To cast doubt that a person is not, or should not, be experiencing life any differently is one way to create more division and anger.
2. Reading and learning from people who have similar faith systems, such as Benjamin Watson. His book, *Under Our Skin*, completely obliterated my defenses and woke me up! His thoughtfulness and background made one amazing story of why it's important for we who profess to love Jesus Christ, to

seek unity in His Name. Reading his story allowed me to see life through the perspective of a Person Of Color instead of only through my own eyes. I keep this book close for reminders. I honestly look up to his family's example. If you do not have a Black or Brown friend to talk to about any of these issues, Watson's book would be a great place to start if you are interested in the "whys" that seem so hard to relate/grasp on our own as White people.

3. Loving Z and his mother, Keesha. I taught Z in the fifth grade, and I loved this silly, active boy fiercely. His mom raised him by herself and since the first time I met her, I have been in awe of her parenting skills. She is not afraid to tackle tough issues, share truth, or even let the ignorant show their true colors. But as much as they mean to me, it was the fear of Z not coming home because an officer might make quick judgments about him and hurt him that opened my eyes to a fraction of the fear moms have for their Black and Brown sons all over our country. God gave me a glimpse of this reality through Z and Keesha. It was triggered when she shared he was old enough to get his driving permit... *all the news stories and sobbing mothers sharing their stories grabbed my heart instead of my defenses*. Does that make sense?

Along the way, I've learned that it's the relationships we have with others, especially the relationships with those who are different from us, that will help us grow the most. Those close relationships help move us past our defensive behavior when we hear the words "White people." Instead of denying we are racist, those relationships can help open our eyes and ears. Instead of focusing on ourselves and all the reasons we are innocent, we see how our friends have faced discmination and it angers us! When those we love are hurt by racism, it becomes a problem we take on, too.

A colleague asked me why I was so obsessed with race reconciliation, and at the time, I could not articulate what was going on inside of me. But God has been working in me this whole time. As much as I love my students, He loves them so much more! So much, that He wants me to see them, understand them, and appreciate the beautiful people He designed and loves. As so many in our society refuse to accept that racism is alive and well, this lie continues to hold back many of His beloved. He gave me the desire and boldness to seek unity and to help others who want it, too.

SIGNS OF HOPE

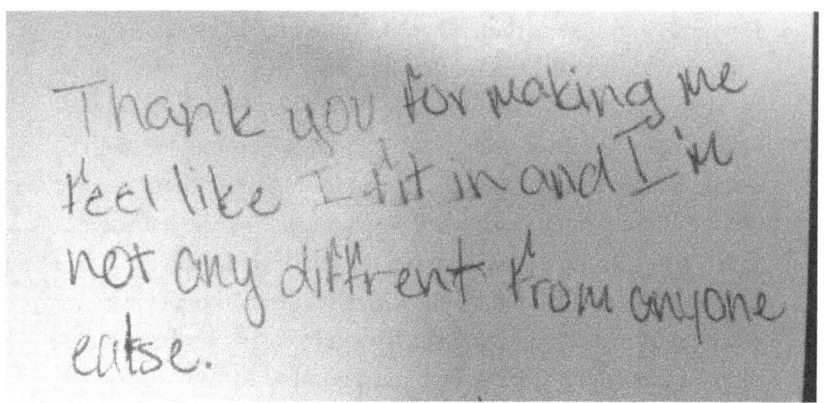

The last year I taught fifth grade, I asked some of my Students Of Color how I could improve my teaching for other Students Of Color in the future. One sweet young lady told me this was the first year she didn't feel as if she were treated differently than others. She felt like she could be herself for the first time in her educational journey. This inspired me to keep growing, but it also hurt my heart knowing it took so long for her to feel accepted in our educational system. Not long after this conversation with my student, my principal assigned me to teach first grade for the next school year. I was excited to help younger students see their value earlier in their educational journey. A decision was made that my students would not leave my class without knowing their worth.

Another thing that gives me hope is that both of my school-aged children had strong, Women Of Color as teachers and loved them! This is different from my own childhood. The friendships we have, now, gives me hope for all of our roles in unity! My children do not see different shades of color as a barrier but rather as something they honor and accept as part of their friendship. I would not be surprised if they grew up to date or marry someone of a different color, nor would I discourage it.

The last thing that gives me hope is finding willing educators to talk about this on Twitter and other social media. I met another educator in my district and was the local President of the Garland Area of Black School Educators and asked me to join. We've had lengthy discussions personally, and the meetings have also opened my eyes to what is necessary to help bring more equitable measures into our system such as supporting our Black teachers, and making sure our parents know how to help their children get into gifted classes and how to advocate for their children.

ACTION STEPS

If you are wanting to be a more culturally responsive educator, there are some steps that can help you get there. I will put them in a logical order but life isn't so logical so don't worry if your journey doesn't look exactly like mine.

1. Google "Systemic racism" and read about it, everything you can. Acknowledge it is real and very much alive in our public school system. Be purposeful in finding a way to be a change agent.
2. Seek out Friends of Color who are willing to share their experiences and believe them. Their stories will not be like your stories. Do not discount their life experiences. Listen more than you speak. Ask questions.
3. Acknowledge your prejudice. Honestly reflect on thinking patterns, implicit bias, and other choices you make in a snap that can hurt People of Color and perpetuate stigma and trauma. Willingly acknowledge where you have been wrong.
4. Do better every day. Become an ally. Stand with People of Color as they fight for real equality. Forget about the politics and media, stand with the real people in your life. There are

times when we will be in silent support standing side by side, and there are times when we will need to use our voices to be loud and heard. Knowing the difference comes with time and wisdom and living out a true belief that we can make changes in our society and school system.
5. As educators, form relationships with your students and their families. Ask for feedback from them. Respect their values and ask for their input. If something doesn't feel right to them about what you are doing, listen and stop before you cause more trauma.
6. Support your Black and Brown colleagues. They often feel outnumbered by their White peers and feel like they can't speak up without being labeled as angry. Listen to them and learn from them how you can support their needs. Join a group that supports Black teachers. Don't be afraid to be the only White person in the room or conversation. It can be scary at first to share what you are learning, and many might ignore or question you, but embrace it. There will be others who you will inspire to join and learn, too.

This journey is not cut and dry. This journey is uncomfortable, painful at times, but rewarding when it plays out in the large scale. We need more people to acknowledge the wrongdoings of our history for all People of Color and how it has repeated itself—even as we have tried to do better. Be the ally. Your students, and our future depend on it.

Melody McAllister

ABOUT THE AUTHOR

Melody McAllister began teaching in Texas in 2004 and has taught first, fifth, and fourth grades in the public school system. She homeschooled her oldest child in Kindergarten and now returns to being a

Home Educator after the recent move to Anchorage, Alaska. She will be teaching preschool, first grade, third, and fifth grades to her children. She and her husband have five children. McAllister is a contributing author for *The Fire Within: Lessons From Defeat that Have Inspired a Passion for Learning* by Mandy Froehlich. She is a recipient of the 2017 Garland NAACP Educator of the Year, and her first children's book will be on the market this fall, titled *I'm Sorry Story* by EduMatch Publishing. She is also the Logistics Manager for EduMatch Publishing and manages the social media sites and the EduMatch Publishing Facebook Community. McAllister is a member of ISTE and most recently spoke in Philadelphia about using technology to promote diversity and inclusion in the classroom.

PART THREE: PREPARING FOR THE FUTURE

HOW TO PREPARE STUDENTS FOR THEIR FUTURE?

Mario Christiner

The story of how my journey to self-discovery led me to the realization that education fails to prepare students for the future. Thus, I created Thrive a social impact startup to hopefully address this global issue.

SELF DISCOVERY

Growing up we all have grand visions of our future selves. As a child, I dreamed of being an inventor, inspired by my idols Benjamin Franklin and Nikola Tesla. During my free time, I was often dissecting electronics and exploring the magical world of electricity. Then as I entered my senior year I was dismayed to discover there was no such thing as an 'Inventor Degree'. For months I leafed through books and spent hours online trying to find the closest degree and choose a university. The vast amount of options was truly overwhelming. Although many fields seemed interesting, I had little idea of how a career in each one would actually be like. Up until that point my work experience ranged from summer camp counselor, babysitter, math tutor, and shoveling snow. Eventually, I decided to study electrical engineering at Worcester Polytechnic Institute (WPI).

My experience at WPI was incredible! The most memorable were the required projects: Interactive Qualifying Project (IQP) and Major Qualifying Project (MQP). For my IQP, I got my first chance to be a leader of a four student group researching the feasibility of rooftop wind turbines in Boston. Then for my MQP, I explored my love for solar energy by prototyping a multi-axis solar tracker. Also, during my studies, I embraced my independence and learned the skills needed to live on my own. However, outside of the projects, I only gained work experience as a tutor, since I did not have a US work permit.

Finally, my bachelor came to an end in 2010 and it was time to start working. I returned to Switzerland to start a year long internship at ABB an international engineering firm focused on energy and automation. At ABB I learned that most engineering work involved programming and simulations. Shortly after my internship, I started a masters degree to further explore the world of solar energy. Just a year into my masters I realized that electrical engineering wasn't for me. During my bachelor we had many hands-on labs and projects to explore different fields of electronics. My new work experience made me realize the majority of the work as an electrical engineer is virtual and focuses on a niche area. Thus I was faced with figuring out what was the right career for me?

In the spring of 2013, I packed my bags and moved to Barcelona in the hope to find myself. Although my future was still unclear, I was excited to explore my options. During my four years in Barcelona I had the chance to work a wide range of jobs. Here are just a few:

- Project manager at a translation company (1 month)
- Blogger for a tourism company (1 month)
- Tour guide for a hostel (1 month)
- Freelance English teacher (2 years)
- Instructor for an after-school robotics program (1 year)

During this time I learned how to network, market myself, and other valuable work skills. I also discovered how rewarding it felt to work with youth, which sparked my transition into education.

For the final part of my self-discovery, I got the opportunity to work as a curriculum developer for a robotics after-school program in Toronto. Here I learned to design experiential learning activities and classes. I also realized how the different stages of child/youth development relate to a student's learning abilities. Yet, there was still something missing in my career.

While in Barcelona I also explored the startup scene. Startups always intrigued me, since it resonated with my initial desire to become an inventor. However, I was discouraged by the fact that the success of startups was determined by their profit and financial valuation. That's why I was excited to learn about social entrepreneurship, which focuses on a social problem and finds a balance of making an impact vs making a profit.

Although the idea of social entrepreneurship was exciting, I was still unsure of what problem to focus on. While living in Toronto I started reflecting on my self-discovery journey and my experiences along the way. What I realized was that many high school and university students shared my challenge of finding their purpose and career path. Finally, at the start of 2019 I launched my own social impact startup Thrive (ThriveSDG.com), which will be further explained at the end.

QUESTIONING EDUCATION

Why should you as an educator care about my self-discovery journey? It took me eight years, over seven jobs, and four countries to discover my calling. Throughout this whirlwind of a journey I learned the majority of the life skills and knowledge needed for work outside of my education, including my bachelor. That begs the question; what is the purpose of education?

You may be skeptical and think my situation is unique. Consider the people you know, how many work in the same field they studied? One example that sparked my doubts about education was during one of my odd jobs facilitating an SAT preparation class with 15 students at an international baccalaureate school in Barcelona. When I asked the students about their future plans only one had a clear idea, all the others were undecided or still choosing between different majors. Furthermore, when talking to post-secondary graduates, I have frequently heard them say how frustrated they are when employers prefer candidates with work experience. Yet, how many students around the world have the opportunity to get relevant work experience before graduating?

It is this gap between education and work that inspired me to start Thrive. Many people may believe the education between kindergarten and high school is meant to prepare students for higher education. So this would mean higher education prepares students for work. However, when do high school students get the chance to explore different career options, so they can make a thought out choice of which career path to choose? And when do students learn the life and career skills they'll need to succeed?

My strong belief is that education's purpose should be to prepare students for their life and career. An education should provide students with the knowledge, experience, and skills to be successful in life. Based on that, let's dig into what is missing in education for the careers of today and the future.

THE EDUCATION GAP

If we wish to understand the gap between education and careers a good place to start is to look at the shift in technology and careers over time. Until the industrial revolution, the majority of work was physical labour, such as farming, to cover basic survival needs. Only a handful of workers were skilled workers creating crafts or offering services. With the start of the industrial revolution in the 18th Century the workforce started to shift into manufacturing jobs. Around this time, mandatory schooling developed in various countries in Europe and North America.

Starting in the 19th Century careers shifted again thanks to electricity. Around 1900 work in the service sector started growing in Europe and North America. At the same time there was a decline in work in the agriculture and manufacturing sectors. Since 2015 more than 80% of the workforce is employed in the service sector. This is shown in the graphic, in which the top part are the percent of service jobs in the US, the middle are manufacturing jobs, and the remaining part are agricultural jobs.

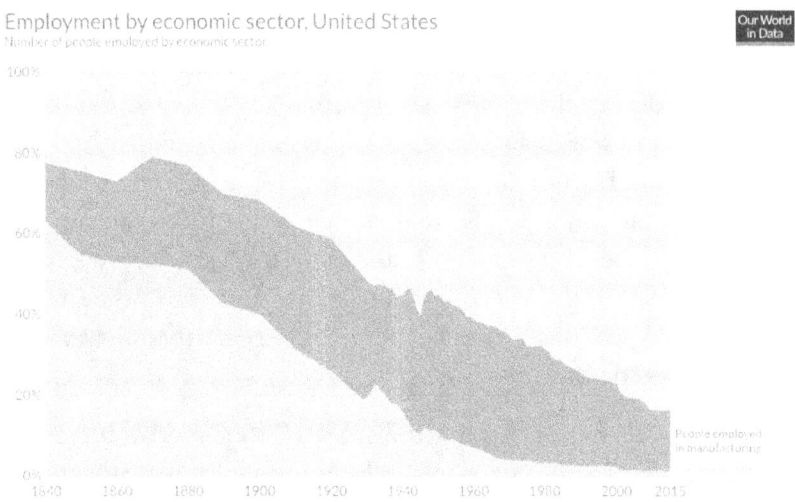

Source: ourworldindata.org

Why is this shift so important? Both agriculture and manufacturing work rely mostly on physical labor. For most service work there is a need for skilled labor that requires thinking and working together with others. This likely correlates with the growth of higher education in the US during the 20th Century.

Another reason for the growth of the service sector were the invention of the computer and the internet. These two technologies have greatly shifted the demand of workers with technical ability and sparked the demand for STEM-related degrees.

So how has education reacted over time? In higher education, the different degrees offered have clearly evolved. The question is, what about primary and secondary education? Since the dawn of formal education, the same subjects have been offered: math, science, language, and history. Depending on the country and school other subjects like art, technology, physical education, etc. have been added to the curriculum. However, if you look at the subjects of standardized rankings, like PISA, the main foci are typically on math, science, and language. The only change has been that STEM-related subjects like math and science are now valued higher.

So why in the 21st Century is education still focused on the same subjects as during the industrial revolution? Think of some of the current fields of work: business, engineering, and government. Yes, the main school subjects still relate to jobs in these fields. However, consider the last time you did some elaborate math, wrote an important email, or wanted to know a historical fact. Most likely you used a spreadsheet, used spell check, or Googled the fact. With the support of technology, we should consider if it makes sense that education is still so focused on these subjects.

You may recall my in-depth self-discovery story at the beginning. Thanks to all my life experiences, I have learned to network to find work, market myself to grow my business, and deal with all sorts of personal challenges along the way. So how can we shift our education to better prepare our students for their future?

FUTURE READY STUDENTS

In order to keep up with the shifts in careers and technology, it's vital that education change. Realistically, we can only attempt to predict the skills and knowledge needed for the future. So I believe that education should empower students to be self-directed learners so that they can quickly learn skills they need for their career along the way. This will also foster students to become lifelong learners and be able to easily adapt to any shifts in careers or new technology.

Students should be provided structure and guidance, but at some point in secondary education, they should be allowed the freedom to adapt their own interests and needs. Why is this flexibility so important?

Currently, most education including higher education provides a structured schedule of when and what students learn. Life is far more chaotic and each individual must be able to take control of their life. From my experience, I've seen people of all ages struggle with time management and prioritizing. A great way to offer this flexibility is by offering more open-ended projects. Using learning videos and flipping the classroom can allow students to choose when and what they learn.

Finally, there is so much value in experiential learning. For any type of work people must combine both theory and practical application. Most life and career skills one can only effectively learn by doing. Again projects are a great way for students to learn by doing. In many projects design thinking can be used to enrich the learning experience. Design thinking allows for iterations, which promotes reflection and promotes good self-learning habits. Using design thinking also develops students' critical thinking, problem-solving, communication, and collaboration skills. Students will likely need all these skills in their lives and careers.

Another great way to prepare students for the future is giving them the chance to explore and solve different real-world problems. Consider some of the problems you've faced in your life, what skills and knowledge did you need to solve each? One way to approach this is by introducing the UN's Sustainable Development Goals (SDGs) to your students. In 2015 the 193 members of the United Nations agreed to achieve 17 SDGs by 2030. These goals address global problems like climate change, inequality, violence, etc. The reason the SDGs are so powerful is that they relate to problems students are currently experiencing or will experience in the future.

As mentioned earlier my self discovery journey and realizing the gaps in education inspired me to launch my own social impact startup Thrive (ThriveSDG.com). We offer curriculum and teacher training to empower high school students to find their purpose and develop their life skills by using design thinking to take on problems related to the UN's Sustainable Development Goals.

At the moment we offer SDG programs that are one month, three month and a year long. At the start of all our programs students learn about the different SDGs and get to explore problems related to each through discussion and mini-challenges. Next students form teams and each team focuses on a particular SDG problem to focus on. For the remainder of the program students use design thinking, a problem-solving method, to take on their problem.

Design thinking is broken into five steps: empathize, define, ideate, prototype, and test. For the one month program students use the first three steps up until ideate. For the other programs students learn and go through all the steps. At the start, students are taught how to do online research to dive deep into their problem. At the end of the research they must create a problem statement that addresses the 5 W's; what is the problem, who it impacts, where the problem is most serious, why it's important, and when the problem started and its evolution over time.

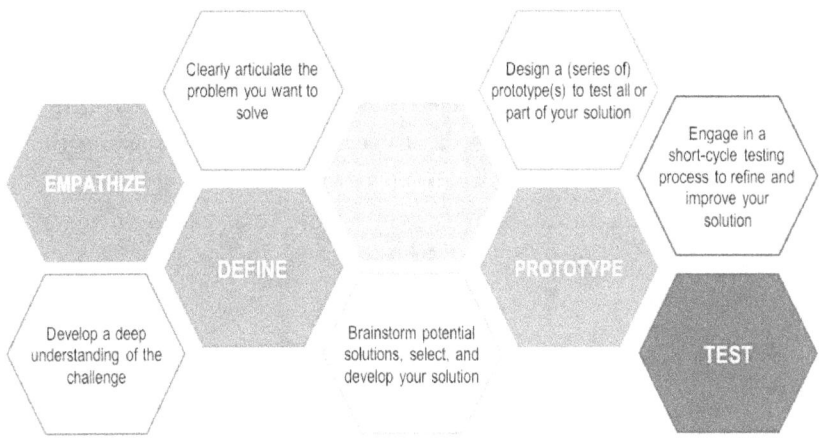

Source: stanford.edu

Once the team has a solid understanding of the problem they brainstorm possible solutions to solve it. They are taught different brainstorm methods, like using mind maps. During this stage they also learn the importance of respecting and building on each others ideas in a constructive way. Afterwards they develop an action plan to implement their solution. In the longer programs students also get the chance to create a tech or social service prototype. During the testing stage teams are supported by the school to try out their solution either at school, in their community, or possibly partnering with a business. Finally, each team creates a video pitch that explains their problem, their learnings, and their solution.

The main outcome of the Thrive program is that students are encouraged to explore problems that potentially lead to a fulfilling career path. Even if only some students find their purpose, it will still encourage students to explore their career options earlier and be better suited to pick a major to study after high school. Finally, all students will develop valuable life skills such as critical thinking, communication, creativity, and teamwork to solve any real-world problem they may encounter.

Thrive is just one option to better prepare students for their future.

Most important is that students get exposed to real-world problems, develop life-skills, and be ready to learn on their own. To achieve this realistically education must change drastically to keep up with the fast paced evolution of technology and careers. If you are reading this I hope you agree that as educators we have a responsibility to prepare students for their future. So what will you do this year to ensure your students are future ready?

Mario Christiner

ABOUT THE AUTHOR

Mario is a global citizen that has lived in both Europe and North America. Starting as an electrical engineer he has since transitioned into the world of education inspired by his love for working with youth. He also believes that education is the key to making the world a better place. Most of his experience has been in non-traditional learning settings as a tutor, mentor, private english teacher, and after-school robotics program facilitator. Since 2017 he has been working as a curriculum developer and recently launched his own startup Thrive (ThriveSDG.com).

Outside work he is a competitive marathon runner, nature enthusiast, culture explorer, sustainability advocate, and knowledge seeker. He's always up for a good chat with like-minded people so feel free to connect with him on Twitter or LinkedIN (@mpchristiner).

PREPARING FOR THE FUTURE

Rachelle Dene Poth

What do educators need to know as we look to the future?

As an educator of 25 years, I have experienced a lot of changes in education. Thinking back to when I was a student, things are so different now and I would never have imagined how much the world would change, especially when it comes to education. Now we are hearing about new methods, new technologies, and new ideas for doing what is best for our students. In my time as a student, the goals were all the same—work toward obtaining a college degree, do well on tests, complete all of your homework, pay attention in class, and then decide your future and next steps. Today, these topics tend to fall into very active discussions in different educator communities. The most popular discussions tend to focus on teaching methods, defining the classroom "space," homework and grading policies, behavior management, and whether students need a college degree to be successful in the future.

I am a curious learner and once I start to hear discussions like these, I want to know more in order to understand both sides or all sides of the discussion. So a little more than a year ago, I started to do some research into the topics that I had been reading more about and did not fully understand their connection to education, nor what I needed to know as an educator. The topics were things like the gig economy, artificial intelligence, machine learning, and place-based learning to name a few. I had a general understanding or a guess of the meaning of most of them, but I was not too sure about the concept of a "gig economy." Wanting to find out fast, I turned to Google and within 30 seconds, I had more than 35 million results. That in itself still amazes me every single time I do a search on the Internet, especially when I think back to all of the hours I have spent in the library searching through card catalogs and stacks of books, hoping to find something and coming up with nothing. Of course with so many results, we still need the right skills to process the information.

After a more advanced search, the concept of a gig economy made sense. It refers to jobs or work assignments which are short-termed and the equivalent of a "gig." We see a lot of examples of this with jobs that tend to employ freelancers or independent contractors rather than full-time employees. To dig a little deeper, I continued my search by narrowing the date to the past year and looking for the top "gig economy" jobs. A few common themes emerged, which then led me to more terms that I was unfamiliar with. Some of the list included: Deep Learning (AI and machine learning), Bitcoin, and Blockchain. Employment in these different and emerging areas is increasing which means that not only do we need to help our students develop a variety of skills, "21st-century skills" for the changing landscape of work, but we need to prepare ourselves too. We have to actively seek information to stay current with trends so that we can help our students develop the skills they need and confidently head toward the future.

But how do we know where to begin? There is so much information available but our time to explore is limited. We cannot possibly know everything, so the best we can do is to know enough to get our students started and then let them lead and teach us too. We can start by offering specific types of learning experiences for all students.

To decide what types of experiences, we can start by looking at data and statistics that are available and we also stay connected with other educators who are working with the same challenges. There were some interesting statistics in regard to the employment of freelancers. In 2016, there were 55 million people[1] working as freelancers who earned on average 17% more per hour than full-time employees. More and more companies are planning to hire freelancers rather than full-time employees. In 2016, 35% of workers were freelancers and it leads me to wonder what that number be in another 10 or 20 years? And what are the skills that these freelancers will need and the technologies that they will need to understand?

WHAT EXPERIENCES WILL HELP?

We cannot know enough, so we need to prepare students for their future by offering innovative and challenging learning experiences. Experiences that will push their problem solving, critical thinking, creativity and collaboration skills and that involve real-world experiences.

Entrepreneurial Courses: How can educators best prepare students for a gig economy workforce or to possibly become entrepreneurs? By designing learning experiences where students have an opportunity to explore, create, and innovate and have choices in the how, what, and where they learn, we will offer more possibilities for inquiry-based learning and foster a growth mindset. Some schools offer programs and courses which lend themselves to these types of possibilities for students.

In my school, we have a course on entrepreneurship, sports and entertainment management, and a variety of STEAM courses where students design problems to solve and explore emerging technologies. A few years ago, one of our business teachers, Patsy Kvortek, recognized a need for more courses that would prepare students for future success. She created a course in "Entrepreneurship" and "Sports and Entertainment Management" and has built-in real-world experiences and project-based learning into the course curriculum. Students learn about real-world tasks such as project management, business management, leveraging social media, planning and tracking finances and how to plan large scale events. I've had many conversations with students in her classes and their excitement for what they are learning and how it is making an impact on them is always obvious. In courses like this and others like it, students are developing skills that will prepare them for many career options, building critical skills of communication, collaboration, problem-solving and as an added benefit, SEL (Social and Emotional Learning) skills as well.

WHAT OTHER TYPES OF LEARNING EXPERIENCES DO STUDENTS NEED?

When it comes to hands-on, student-driven learning that promotes student interests, project-based learning is something that all students should experience. In a keynote given by Alan November, international keynote speaker and author, he said that educators must "teach students how to learn." He also stated: "I think we should begin to move more and more toward the skill side, because if we teach you to memorize and regurgitate content and your job is wiped out by technology, you're not well prepared to reinvent yourself if you didn't learn how to learn."

Reading through November's message and reflecting on the changes that I have seen in education during my career as a whole and also during the past five years reinforces the importance for students to have opportunities to learn to communicate, collaborate, problem-solve, and think critically. These key skills will benefit students regardless of what they decide to do after high school, whether they enroll in college, start a job, pursue specialized training, or maybe even take a gap year to explore the world before making a decision about their future.

Project-based learning (PBL) gives students the chance to design their own learning path without a specific direction to go in, nor only one right answer, if any, to find. With PBL, students experience and engage in sustained inquiry, they learn to focus on the process of learning and developing their skills of creativity, critical thinking, and problem-solving. Beyond that, at times, students experience the productive struggle that comes with learning and build perseverance as they work through it. When students have more real-world experiences, such as through PBL or even place-based learning, they make more authentic and meaningful connections with what they are learning about. It matters more to them. When students can learn and build skills by volunteering at community centers, traveling to rural areas or a city to identify and solve problems like cleaning up the environment, starting a recycling program, or planting a garden, they become better at brainstorming ideas, collaborating with peers and building connections beyond the classroom.

STEM AND EMERGING TECHNOLOGIES

We are at that time where technology changes so rapidly that we may in fact need to shift our focus from understanding every aspect of a specific tech tool or trend, and instead seek to understand the skills that are required and opportunities that arise as a result of these technologies. We also need to think about the application of these concepts and technologies to the future of education and the future of work.

Courses that blend in STEM or STEAM curriculum will help teachers to provide ways for students to build the core skills that they need, especially when it comes to learning about technology. Students need to understand how things work, how to iterate and design new technologies. Even in a world where there are countless apps available, many of which complete complex tasks, we still need humans to keep our technology relevant and competitive.

Educators can facilitate greater, more personalized learning experiences for students by fostering a "STEM mindset" in students. As Dr. Jacie Maslyk, assistant superintendent and author of books on STEAM and makerspaces, "The way we engage with our students can build confidence and fuel curiosity." In a world where the future of learning and work are uncertain, the best way to provide for our students is to push their curiosity, promote risk-taking and challenge them to explore emerging technologies and different STEM concepts and be there to support them along the way.

ARTIFICIAL INTELLIGENCE

A topic that has caught my attention and influenced me to do a lot of research and even enroll in a course to learn more is Artificial Intelligence. Last fall, I was fortunate to enroll in the ISTE U course on artificial intelligence, where I gained new perspectives on AI, how it will impact the world of education and work, and gathered many new teaching tools for use with my students. For a great resource, I recommend Michelle Zimmerman's book, *Teaching AI: Exploring New Frontiers for Learning*. It was a tremendous help when working through the course and building my knowledge base.

Discussion about AI and its uses in all sectors of work and in education is constant. A recent estimate that I heard was that 40% of jobs will be replaced by AI in the not-to-distant future. Knowing this, how can we prepare our students to be competitive with AI and to also understand its capabilities so that students can do more than consume, but instead can become the creators and innovators?

WHERE DO WE SEE AI?

It is amazing what technology can do and the instant access that it provides to information. I did a quick search on Google of "artificial intelligence" and it turned up 615 million results in .82 seconds. Wow! Sorting through the results does not give the best or most accurate definition or examples of Artificial Intelligence. I filtered my search and came across a project called #AskAboutAI, a research project started by Getting Smart. Through their research, they identified over 100 applications of AI to life in areas such as recreation, transportation, education, healthcare, gaming and many others. Here are some of the ways we interact with AI daily.

Communication: AI is used to streamline the amount of spam through the filters and continues to learn over time as you mark additional items as spam.

Travel: Driving apps such as Uber or Lyft use Machine Learning, a form of AI. One fact that surprised me is that in the airline industry, it is estimated that "human steered" flight time is only seven minutes of actual flight length, leaving the rest to auto-pilot which is AI.

Social networks: Most people are engaging in some form of social media use. Facebook shared results of how successful AI is at detecting spam but not as successful with detecting hate speech or cyberbullying. AI completes face detection each time you add photos and see a name pop up for photo tagging.

Shopping: Services like Amazon use AI to analyze your prior data and make suggestions based on your preferences over time.

Fraud protection. There are systems in place that analyze your purchasing trends and location, and will immediately flag something if it considers it to be an uncommon transaction. It works fast, sending an alert and can also cancel the transaction immediately.

BUT WHAT CAN AI DO FOR EDUCATION?

There is so much information out there, overwhelming at times, and becoming an instant expert is not too likely because the information and technologies change so rapidly. Each day there are news alerts of AI and how it is being used in education and in other sectors of work. While we may not become experts, we can use this as an opportunity to keep on learning and pushing ourselves to stay current and relevant so we can provide the best opportunities for our students. By doing this, we can take the information we find and use it as a starting point of inquiry with our students, because chances are they'll be interacting with AI in the future wherever they decide to go after their high school careers. There is also the likelihood that they will be working alongside AI in the future in some capacity.

Regardless of the teaching methods or technologies we choose to explore and use in our classrooms and schools, we have to keep focused on the purpose. What will the benefits be of implementing PBL or place-based learning? What are the benefits of the technology, in this case, AI, and how practical is it to use? Time is always a concern and when it comes to providing authentic, meaningful and personalized learning experiences for our students, we need to make the most of our time. There are many tasks that go along with teaching and that tends to take away some of the time we can spend getting to know and work with our students. This is where I believe that AI can truly make an impact for good.

Students can have access to virtual tutors that meet their schedules and enroll in online courses that are taught by AI. These capabilities expand the how, when and where they can learn. Knowing how to code becomes a skill that is marketable to many areas. Students will possibly become the next app designers, create new innovations, while developing the critical "21st century" skills that they need to be successful in whatever their goals may be. Some schools in the country are now offering courses in AI. In Pittsburgh, the Montour School District launched the country's first middle-school AI program in 2018. Justin Aglio, Director of Innovation, has shared a lot of the work that students are doing and I had the opportunity to visit the school and see for myself what some of the capabilities are. It was great to interact with students and hear from them about the possibilities with AI, ones that I had not considered.

A FEW POSSIBILITIES THAT I CAN SEE ARE:

Students and teachers will be able to connect and have access instantly with resources that meet their needs at the moment they need them. AI will be able to make decisions by analyzing responses and interactions and then provide immediate access to a world full of resources to each student and teacher.

Assessments: AI will help to save time in the grading process and how we create and use assessments. With AI we can provide differentiated instruction that will adjust in real-time as students work through class materials. AI is able to analyze the data faster and provide information for teachers to act upon and work with each student.

STAYING INFORMED

We start by planning different opportunities for students to explore AI to find something that interests them and then empower them to become the creators. It is more than simply knowing how it works or the benefits it may provide, we need to help our students learn how to code, to design new technologies that will make an impact for our future. There are debates about the ethics behind AI, how can it be used for good, will AI replace teachers, and many more concerns. But if we think back to every great new technology discovery over the years, they all came with some element of controversy and concern. We address those concerns and stay focused on the why behind using it and continue to evaluate and reflect on our practice.

CALL TO ACTION

Be intentional in planning experiences that will foster the skills of adaptability, resilience and persistence.

Seek learning opportunities that will promote the development of skills such as problem-solving, critical thinking, collaboration, and communication.

Understand the new trends impacting education and work. (AI, AR/VR, gig economy, entrepreneurship).

Create ways for students to become risk-takers as they design their own learning journeys.

Give students the space to design their own learning path and to take charge of their education.

Rachelle Dene Poth

ABOUT THE AUTHOR

I am a Spanish and STEAM: What's nExT in Emerging Technology Teacher at Riverview Junior Senior High School in Oakmont, PA. I am also an attorney and earned my Juris Doctor Degree from Duquesne University School of Law and have a Master's Degree in Instructional Technology. I serve as President of the ISTE Teacher Education Network and the Communications Chair for the ISTE Mobile Learning Network.

I received the Making IT Happen Award and a Presidential Gold Award for volunteer service to education during the ISTE 2019 Conference. I was selected as the 2017 Outstanding Teacher of the

Year by PAECT (the Pennsylvania Association for Educational Communications in Technology, the PA affiliate of ISTE) and by the NSBA as one of the "20 to Watch."

I am the author of *In Other Words: Quotes That Push Our Thinking* and *Unconventional*, both published by EduMatch, and T*he Future is Now: Looking Back to Move Ahead*, published by Edugladiators.

LEARNING WITH IOT

David J. Lockett

The Internet of Things refers to a connected group of physical devices that can exchange data and thus interact with the physical world in an enhanced way. The Internet of Things has vastly improved efficiency and convenience for its users, connecting our lives and our devices in an unprecedented way. These networks would not be possible without high-quality STEM education and talented individuals who have observed our technological needs and developed these complex systems.

The merits of STEM-related careers are many. Careers in these disciplines are often associated with significant worker satisfaction, sizeable incomes, and potential for career growth. However, these careers are important for more than just those who choose those careers. Having people excel in STEM helps our entire society because people in STEM careers provide us with essential STEM-related security, the daily conveniences that STEM products afford, and an economy that can keep up with the rest of the world.

A major challenge for educators has been getting students excited about STEM careers. Some educators and policymakers rely on rational arguments to get students interested and motivated in STEM. However, demonstrating the fascinating outcomes created by STEM professionals is a more compelling way to engage students. Not only is IoT a product of STEM, but it enables activities that students are likely both fascinated by and appreciate—including activities related to learning, security, and monitoring.

The concept of the Internet is more intuitive for today's students than for previous generations, as students have grown up relying on the Internet in an age where the Internet is ubiquitous. Students are using Internet-connected devices like smartphones and laptops regularly, including in the classroom and so have the fundamental knowledge and experience to help them understand IoT. Not only do they use these devices, but they also report liking them and wanting more of them in the classroom. Thus, if shown how physical devices can be interconnected into a network—and the associated benefits—it is likely that students would become enthusiastic about IoT.

Pointing out the IoT that students enjoy in their daily lives is a great way to introduce them to IoT and to get them interested in pursuing relevant careers. In the classroom, IoT helps prevent grading errors and lost homework and increases efficiency. It may even help with classroom security. Between the various devices, apps, and robots that rely on IoT, the possibilities are endless for gaining the attention of those students who are not impressed by the benefits of IoT.

Introducing students to IoT is critical for ensuring that our students continue to stay at the forefront of STEM developments. By creating an IoT classroom, with devices such as whiteboards and lights connected through the Internet, teachers can show students how IoT can enhance learning and improve the day-to-day experience of school while cutting down costs and enhancing classroom safety. By connecting with students based on their specific interests and hobbies, educators can better motivate these students to pursue the study of STEM and IoT.

REFERENCE

Hung, M. Leading the IoT. 2017(2).

David J. Lockett

PREPARING STUDENT TEACHERS WITH A SPRINKLE OF EDUMAGIC

Dr. Sam Fecich

Hello friends!

After working with EduMatch to publish *EduMagic: A Guide for Preservice Teachers,* I knew that there had to be more to the story focusing on student teachers. Enter stage right – preparing future teachers for student teaching with a sprinkle of EduMagic! I decided to break this chapter up into several sections:

- Preparing for student teaching—focusing on stuff that you can do the semester (or summer) before you student teach.
- Rocking it during student teaching—ideas and strategies to help you slay your student teaching.
- Reflecting on your student teaching—tying it all together and showcasing your learning.

Let's jump in!

PREPARING FOR STUDENT TEACHING

Let me begin this section by stating you are ready for this. If you weren't ready for student teaching, you wouldn't be doing it. You know your stuff, you have read and studied your material, you have had several teaching experiences before this event, and you got this. You are strong. Please keep in mind throughout your journey of student teaching that this is practice. Student teaching is practice for you to know what it is like to be a teacher day in and day out.

The next few strategies are some things that you can do the semester or summer before you student teach. One way to help you prepare for student teaching is to reach out to your mentor or cooperating teacher. Send an email to your cooperating teacher introducing yourself to him or her. Here are some highlights you can include in your intro email to your cooperating teacher:

- Name and major (obvi)
- Your teaching story—why you want to be a teacher or who inspired you to become a teacher
- What you like to do outside of classes and studying. For example, share what your interests, hobbies, and extracurriculars are outside of school.
- When is a good time for you to visit their classroom to observe and meet in person. You may want to include some dates/times that work for you. You will also want to denote how long you are aiming at meeting with the mentor teacher. If you are wanting to observe the teacher for a few classes, put that in the email. If you just want to do a quick meet and greet and then set up a time to observe at another date/time, share that too. These visits would obviously happen before you official start date, so make sure you reach out to them well before you are supposed to start!

Before you send this email make sure you read it over and fix any mistakes. This is your first impression with this educator, and you want it to be a positive and professional one. Then click send! Sit back and relax—NOT!

SECRETS TO CRAFTING A STUDENT TEACHER LETTER

Now is the time to get started on thinking through what you want to include in your meet the student teacher letter for the students and families in your student teaching class. It is so important to make a connection with students and their families, even if you are the student teacher. Reaching out and informing parents and caregivers is critical. As a student teacher, you play an important role in a child's education, even if it is only for seven weeks. I am sure if you think about it, you can remember one or two student teachers that you may have had in your younger years.

Here are some elements of a "Meet the Teacher" letter or flyer home to parents. A disclaimer though: there are so many ways to write and create this letter, there is definitely no one right way. I want to share with you a few of my favorite elements. Below are some features you will want to include in your letter In some cases I left you some space to write down your ideas for content in each area.

- Teacher-friendly photo: What I mean this is a fun, yet professional photo of you, and just you!
- Teaching story: Share the reason why you teach. Why do you want to impact young lives? Why do you want to be an educator of excellence?
- Background: Think of this section as information about you such as family, where you are from, what you are studying, what you plan to do after graduation, etc.
- Contact information: You may want to put a link to your digital portfolio. You may also want to put something like, "To contact me please contact (insert name of mentor teacher here)."
- Sign it: End it with a signature and how you want to be addressed. Example: Miss Kathy Fry or Mr. Joe Ondash.
- Fun facts or favorites: food, movie, restaurant, ice cream flavor, game, sport, etc. You get the idea, fun facts or hidden talents about you.

Alright, now that you have your ideas and content flowing, let's talk about how to create your own student teacher letter. Here are some that I suggest that are free and user-friendly: Canva, Smore, Microsoft Sway, and Adobe Spark. All of these tools allow you the option to print out copies for each student in your class and/or share the letter (with your cooperating teacher's permission) on the class website. This is a great way to reach out and inform parents about who you are and what you are all about. Just like your email to your cooperating teacher, read it over a few times and fix any mistakes. Please share out a picture of your student teacher letter on social media with #EduMagic.

MEETING YOUR COOPERATING TEACHER

Hopefully by this time your cooperating teacher has gotten back to you, and you're on your way to a meet and greet with your mentor teacher. When you are first meeting your cooperating teacher there are a few things you are going to want to have with you: copies of your clearances to enter the school and a notebook or way to document ideas. When you meet your cooperating teacher, make eye contact and shake their hand, introduce yourself with a clear voice and state the college or university you are representing. For example, "Hi, Mr. Fecich. My name is Sam Smith and I'm your student teacher from Awesome University. Thank you for working with me." This gives the cooperating teacher a quick reminder of who you are and how to pronounce your name.

When you get to the cooperating teacher's classroom, take note of how s/he decorates, has the classroom arranged, organized, etc. Get to know your cooperating teacher a little bit. You may be afraid you may not find someone to click with. It is important to know that you are not going to get along with everyone. Everyone is not going to like you. That is OK. But, let's work on how we can start the relationship on a positive and professional note.

- Tell me your teaching story (and share yours!)
- Why did you become a teacher and what keeps you in the profession?

- What gets you excited about in the field of education?
- What are your expectations of me, and my time with you from this experience?
- What are some ways I can use these first days to get in front of students?
- Find a way to say "This is what I hope to get out of this experience with you…"
- I have seven, eight, or nine weeks and this is what my program recommends that I do…

By setting up the conversation on a professional and positive note it sets the stage for a professional relationship to develop. Now, let's fast forward a few months and get down to it–the main event–student teaching!

ROCKING IT DURING STUDENT TEACHING

The time has come. It is time to student teach. Take a deep breath. You got this! With these tips, you are going to succeed during student teaching. Set yourself up for success before student teaching begins by following a few simple routines:

- Get into a routine the week before you begin student teaching. Meaning set your alarm so you have enough time to get ready. Get to bed at a decent time so you are getting 7-9 hours of rest.
- Take a test drive to the school so you know how long it takes to get there in the morning with traffic. Find alternative routes to the school just in case of weather or construction – or to find a coffee shop to get your morning cuppa tea.
- Pack your teaching bag! Seriously just like you were in elementary school get your teacher bag ready to go with all of your teacher must-haves.

Here some items you are going to want to make sure you have in your bag:

- Teacher mug and reusable water bottle
- Healthy snacks that will get you through the day (trail mix, multigrain bars)
- Notebook
- Sticky notes or index cards
- Pens (a good pen), highlighter, sharpie
- Hand sanitizer and lotion
- Small first aid kit–band-aids, cough drops, Tylenol
- Stain remover stick
- Personal care items–travel toothbrush/toothpaste, mouthwash, deodorant, Chapstick, hair ties, bobby pins, etc.
- Mints
- Charger for phone and laptop

Okay, it may be getting close to when you student teach maybe a month away, and you may be asking yourself, "What should I have in my student teaching binder?" I get this question every year around this time and I am here to share with you some of my go-to areas for a student teacher binder.

ULTIMATE GUIDE TO YOUR STUDENT TEACHING BINDER

A student teacher binder is a must-have, but a well-organized one makes you extra prepared! One edtech tool that I suggest to help you create a beautifully designed and organized student teacher binder is Canva. Canva is a free tool (app and website) that you can use to design your own personalized student teacher binder. There are many templates that you can use to make it just as unique and wonderful as you! Some sections that you are going to want to have in your student teacher binder include (again in no order):

- Contact information for your cooperating teacher and college supervisor
- Name
- Phone number
- Email address

- Classroom number and office number of your supervisor
- Class roster and annotated seating chart - for each period that you teach with start/end times for each period
- School schedule or calendar
- Class schedule
- Calendar (Monthly, so you can see events and concepts at a glance; Weekly, to focus in on those areas each week; and Daily, broken down into times of the day)
- Standards for the subject areas in which you will teach
- Lesson plans separated for each subject area and a place to reflect
- Professional development log (Topic, Date/Time, Big ideas or takeaways from the session)

Additionally, have on hand procedures, those that you observe and/or ask your cooperating teacher to document for you. Common classroom procedures include:

- How to take and submit attendance
- What to do if a student is late
- How are grades submitted (daily, weekly, etc.)?
- How is feedback provided to students?
- How to take and submit lunch count
- Late assignments and what the steps are to submit late work
- How students enter and exit the classroom
- How students line up to leave
- Fire drills
- Emergency card location
- Where they hand in their homework
- Bathroom policy
- If they finish work early

Friends, this is not by any means an exhaustive list of must-haves for your student teaching binder—just something to get you started. When you are done creating the content for your student teacher binder, print out your materials and put them into plastic sleeves.

Then put those sleeves into your binder. You are going to also want to put some loose-leaf paper into your binder too, so you have plenty of room to take notes during observations. Let's talk about that first day of student teaching.

FIRST DAY OF STUDENT TEACHING

During the first few days, you are going to be doing a lot of observing. I encourage you to also try to observe other classes in your grade level and specials. Inquire if you can try to observe other specialist and classroom environments such as speech, occupational therapy, physical therapy, library, art, music, gym, etc. While you are observing, make sure you have a place to document your learning whether that be a notebook or digitally record some areas of the lesson that were positive, a way to modify it for learners or improve upon it in some way, and one interesting aspect, question, or takeaway. If you are observing your host teacher DO NOT go up to them and tell them what they can improve upon, but do ask them questions about why they chose to deliver the content in such a manner, why they selected the text, or how they evaluated students. This will help you to get to know their strategy and thought behind the activity and methods used. Never be afraid to ask questions, they can only help you. So, if you have questions ask away!

Please don't wait for your teacher to ask you to jump in. Take the initiative and get started on projects you can with the permission of your supervisor. Maybe you can work on the hallway bulletin board or look over late work. If anything, try to get to know your students by building a relationship with them. Know their names and get to know their interests. You can use some of your intel to design lessons and incorporate their hobbies into lessons if you can. Maybe it's the first few days and you are working with your cooperating teacher on planning out your first lesson for the students. It's important to prepare a fully detailed lesson from top to bottom. Hand your lesson plan in with plenty of time for feedback and revision. Think about what kind of feedback do you want from your teacher. Be specific when asking for feedback from your co-op (example question asking in blooms). Be prepared to share how you thought it went and areas that could have been more developed. Then teach that lesson and reflect on how it went.

Hopefully, you get a few lessons under your belt before it is time to teach during a college supervisor. I am going to share with you the supervisor observation secret sauce. Let's get down to it–having a college or university supervisor observe one of your lessons can be super nerve-racking! We get it–we were there once. Yeah, believe it or not we were student teachers too! We all got feedback some good and some not so great. I will split up some ways that you can prepare for your college supervisor visit into three categories. Here we go!

BEFORE THE OBSERVATION

First, make sure that you know how you will be evaluated. Here in Pennsylvania, we evaluate student teachers based on theCharlotte Danielson Framework for Teaching. It has four domains – planning and prep, instruction, classroom environment, and professional responsibilities. When I go into an observation, I have this document up on my laptop and I am writing feedback as it fits into each of those areas. I write about what I observe and how it fits into each of those four domains.

Supervisor secret: I color code my feedback in some cases. If I write something with a dark yellow font that means when I come back to observe the student teacher, I would like to see improvement in that area. I learned that hack from a colleague of mine–it has been very helpful.

Sometimes you know ahead of time if your supervisor will come to see you that day. If you do,have a space ready to go for him/her to observe you teach. Make sure that there is a place for the supervisor to sit so they have a clear view of your teaching and so that they can hear you too. I know it sounds silly, but trust me, they need to have a spot where they can see and hear you work your magic. Usually, this is at the student teacher desk in the classroom. In addition, you are going to want to make sure that you have all materials and lesson plans ready for the supervisor to check out during their observation. So, if you are using a handout and a specific textbook (if there is an extra copy) put it at the desk where your supervisor will be so s/he can follow along.

Sometimes you don't know when your supervisor will be visiting (that is OK). Get in the habit of setting up all of your materials just in case. You never know, and by having these items prepared daily, you will feel more at ease.

Plan a lesson and write the lesson plan! Go all out when planning—especially if this is one of your first observations by your supervisor. Clearly detail each part of the lesson. This is a great way to get feedback on your planning and it will help you out too in the long run.

Show a running record of reflection. Reflection is critical. In my book, EduMagic, I share how reflection saves lives—not just yours but your students too! Reflection is not just putting anything down after a lesson—but really dig deeper than that. Yes, in the moment after a lesson you may want to write a few things down on sticky notes—but after that during lunch or at the end of the day really reflect on the lesson.

1. Did your students meet the objectives?
2. What would you do differently if you were to teach this lesson again?
3. How can you adapt the lesson for a specific student who was struggling?
4. How will you go back and reteach or review this topic in the future?
5. How did you assess your students?
6. How could you tell that your students were engaged in your lesson?

BONUS: Provide feedback from your cooperating teacher! This can help get the conversation going with your supervisor to see where you are having some issues and where you are rockin' it.

DURING THE OBSERVATION

Friends, **DO NOT** put on a dog and pony show for the sake of the supervisor. We want you to do what you do best – TEACH! This part is easy – take a deep breath – smile, you got this, and just TEACH! You can do this—teach a lesson that you prepared for. If it goes wrong that's OK, we will talk about some ways you can fix it or rework it. If it goes right (nothing goes perfect 100% of the time) great too we will talk about that too.

Remember a supervisor is going to be giving you feedback some positive and some areas that need to be worked on during the debrief. Supervisors are going to be looking for the following areas (and more):

1. Do you know your subject area?
2. Are the objectives tied to state or Common Core standards?
3. Are the students engaged in the lesson? How can you tell?
4. Did the students reach the objective?
5. Did the lesson plan make sense in sequence and activities?
6. How is your professional presence in front of students?
7. Does the student teacher show reflection?
8. an the student teacher be flexible in their teaching?

   BONUS: Greet students as they come in the classroom - by name! It pays to know your students and build relationships with them.

AFTER THE OBSERVATION

OK, you just taught a lesson in front of your supervisor–way to go. Take a deep breath. It is done. Maybe it was fantastic, maybe there were a few hiccups, or maybe it just didn't fly. It is OK–you will survive.

Let your supervisor know if you can meet immediately after the observation (with permission from the cooperating teacher).

Take a few minutes before you debrief and think write a sticky note anything that comes to mind for these areas:

1. What features of the lesson went well?
2. What could be improved upon next time you teach this lesson?
3. Something that was interesting or a question you have. Remember this is a time for you to reflect on all the areas of teaching not just on content delivery.

Go into the debrief with an open mind and not on the defensive end. Remember this feedback will help you become a better educator to impact students. We are going to give you specific feedback we may ask clarifying questions or gives descriptions or accounts of specific examples.

Supervisor secret: One question that I love to ask at the end of the observation when I am conferencing with a teacher is, **"What was the objective of the lesson and did the students achieve it–why or why not?"**

Try not to take the feedback personally–I know it's too hard not to do that. Think about the feedback it is to help you be a better teacher.

1. How can you make it better for next time?
2. Where can you go for PD in that area?
3. Is there a resource that your co-op can suggest in this area? Is there an article, a podcast, a webinar that you can attend to help you strengthen that area in your teaching?

Friends, I hope that this episode helped to calm your nerves and get you ready to plan your supervisor's observation with calm and confidence.

You are a guest in the school so step it up a notch in your professionalism like the edumagician that you are! What do I mean by this?

- Dress the part. Dress like a teacher.
- Carry yourself in a professional manner and speak in a way that shows you are an educator.
- Arrive early to your placement.

- Turn in your lesson plans on time to your co-op and supervisor.
- Reflect often on not only content delivery but student engagement, learning, classroom management, behavior management, etc.
- Listen and ask questions.
- Try something new and don't be afraid to take a risk. Meaning, try out a strategy or tech tool you will learn from this experience whether it flies high or flops.

GET INVOLVED OUTSIDE OF SCHOOL

Friends, if you can try to get involved with student life outside of school. Take time to go see the musical, play, or sporting event going on to support your students. Students will notice and they will appreciate it. You will enjoy it too. Make time in your monthly calendar to get involved and attend an event for your students—it will help to foster that connection and relationship. Perhaps your cooperating teacher is a volunteer for an after-school organization or club. Ask if you can help him/her out with activities, events, or planning. Don't just log your time, get in, and get out. Get to know the students, school, and community.

Remember that student teaching is practice. This is the only time you will have another certified teacher in a classroom who has your back so ask and learn. You got this. For those Wizard of Oz fans out there – you have heart, the brains, and the courage to be a student teacher. You have what it takes. You won't get it all right every day, and that is OK you are learning, growing, and practicing what it is like to be an educator of excellence. You will learn so much during this experience. You will learn about yourself, your students, your teaching strategy, your teaching voice, and who you want to become as a teacher, coworker, and student. It's important to document your learning and reflect on this powerful and intense learning experience.

REFLECTING ON YOUR STUDENT TEACHING

So, the journey to and from student teaching is completed. You did it. You survived—now what? Well, maybe you find yourself in one of two boats. The first boat is that steering you into another semester of coursework and you need to switch back into college student mode—wiser, stronger, braver. Or maybe you are in the second boat, the boat that is headed off to graduation toward adulting. Either boat you are in, you still have one thing you need to do before you board. You need to take time to reflect on your experience. Whether it was an amazing experience and brings tears to your eyes or it was lackluster and brings tears to your eyes for a whole other reason you need to debrief and reflect on it. You learned so much during this experience both good and bad that will work to shape you as a new educator. You need to reflect for several reasons:

- Builds your confidence in your experience, some wins of student teaching to speak and some lessons learned.
- Allows you to identify some strong resume points to share.
- Document in a digital portfolio what you did and use it as examples to showcase during an interview.

There is a lot to take in and reflect upon at the end of student teaching. Here are some areas to keep you thinking. You may want to print out this page and put it in your student teacher binder so as ideas come to you, you can document them. You may think you will remember, but trust me friends, write them down. In addition to writing down ideas try to add in examples or small anecdotes that support the idea to help you visualize. Or hey even draw a picture if that helps!

- Planning lessons for daily, weekly content, and units
- Reflection on lessons (delivery, student engagement, did students' meet the objective?)
- Classroom management/school-wide behavior support
- Classroom arrangement
- Behavior management

- Technology tools
- Strategies for when the tech fails
- Teaching strategies or methods (how you taught the topics through activities, group work, etc)
- Routines and procedures what are some that you want to keep for your classroom?
- Organization: are there any organization tips/tricks that you saw used you may want to implement one day.
- List of go-to websites for your content area (or create an awesome Pinterest board)

By reflecting early and often you can use these concepts to shape your digital portfolio and resume. You can showcase your lessons, units, and management strategies through pictures and videos (with appropriate permissions of course). Once you have these created and showcased you can use them to refer to during an interview.

EduMagicians, student teaching is hard. You will have great days that validate why you got into the profession and you will have days where you go home and cry. You will come up against challenges, but there will be plenty to celebrate too. You need to have the good and the bad. Friends, you got this! You are prepared, you know your stuff, you are ready.   Remember, you have the EduMagic in YOU!

Dr. Sam Fecich

ABOUT THE AUTHOR

Hi! I'm Dr. Sam Fecich, a professor of education, author, and a huge fan of pumpkin spice lattes (PSL)! I'm a professor of education at Grove City College where I work with future teachers in areas related to edtech and special ed. I am also the author of *EduMagic: A guide for preservice teachers* and the host of the EduMagic Podcast designed with future teachers in mind. I teach to impact classrooms that I will never see through the work of amazing future educators.

Follow my journey and let's connect!

PART FOUR: TAKING CARE OF OURSELVES (AND EACH OTHER)

#SEL4ADULTS

Brian Kulak (@bkulak11)

We can't help our kids if we don't help ourselves.

They need us more than they want to admit.

After all, they have been trained to ask for help, but only after asking three other friends first. Each day, they are trying new things, remembering old things, laughing and crying with each other. Sometimes they become friends outside of school; sometimes they prefer to stay exclusively school buddies.

We see them help each other when they fall. We see them shoot some side-eye at each other or at us. We try our best to put them in the best possible classes, with the best combination of people, because we so badly want them to succeed every year. We notice when they come to school exhausted or despondent, and we expect them to simply go about their business. "This is a place of learning," we say, "so let's get to it."

We preach the power of the almighty rubric, and we remind them their scores count! Attendance, too! And don't forget to get involved in activities outside the classroom! In fact, we probably say many things that end with a real or assumed exclamation point!

Leaders, our teachers need us more than ever.

What? You thought we were talking about someone else?

As I prepared for my first year as a building leader, I spent last summer poring over leadership articles, theories, and TED talks. I talked to current and former leaders about what makes for a successful school opening. I grilled my daughter about her principal, and I thought about all the leaders who were ever in my orbit. What I got was a combination of buzzword bingo and school-specific advice that was not useful even if I were able to wedge it into my own experience. What I didn't get was any reference to the teachers' well being.

Sure, I know the most important responsibility of any leader is to hire the best possible people. As a former district leader tasked with creating the professional development opportunities for staff, I know meaningful, relevant PD is vitally important. I know at the heart of everything we do is the kids we serve.

But if we mean to truly lead, we have to take care of our teachers. And I don't mean subscribing to a one-size-fits-all style, a panacea for all that ails public education. What I'm suggesting is a shift in how we view ourselves: not as the principal of a building or of our children. Rather, as the leader of our teachers, for all they are and all they are not. We don't get to directly affect the daily growth of the students in our charge, but we can, and should, affect the daily growth of our teachers.

This is the most important part of our job, and frankly, it's the easiest. Here's how.

START WITH HUMILITY

Risky though it may have been, one of the first things I did to introduce myself to staff was to share my Mistakeume. Think of it as a resume of mistakes. Formatted to look and function like an actual resume, this tongue-in-cheek document alerted my new staff to mistakes I made while in my former role. Rather than start the year with all kinds of "ideas to improve" or with a heightened focus on what

I thought of our school and staff, I wanted to make certain they saw me as I am: human and fallible.

Imagine the opposite from a teacher's perspective.

You approach the new year with equal parts excitement and dread. While you can't wait to see the kids, you have the specter of a new leader, who is replacing a highly respected and effective leader, looming over your September start date. A week or two before you are set to return, you receive an email from your new leader, and it's full of edu-jargon, self-important noise, and a robotic, from-the-handbook style. There's nothing genuine or human about the letter. It's a formality. A box checked. A farce.

And an, "Oh, yeah, Welcome Back!"

I am under no illusion that I am above, ahead of, or superior to our staff, but I am aware there are leaders who operate to the contrary. Let me make it simple. If you consider your professional ego with anything but a gross aftertaste in your mouth, you're doing it wrong, and your staff will suffer.

GIVE TIME BACK

Our collective relationship with time is sadly one-sided. We all need more of it, but time just takes and takes, irrespective of who or what it leaves in its wake. So leaders, we can choose to throw our hands up at our powerlessness over time, or we can choose to get creative, refusing to give in.

In our district, our elementary staff has two meetings per month by contract. How we choose to conduct those meetings is not stipulated. This is our first opportunity to sucker punch time right in the gut.

First, rather than assuming or dictating what your staff will do during those two meetings, ask what they *prefer* to do. The asking, in itself, is giving time back because you're considering your staff, their voice, and their time, as equal to or greater than your own.

When I put this out to staff, vocal leaders suggested we keep one meeting in a traditional. Before the meeting, a formal agenda is shared, staff has input toward its completion, and we all meet face to face. Ultimately, getting everyone in the same room is as important as whatever appears on that agenda.

We also commit to closing each traditional meeting with a staff shout out. During this final segment, anyone can shout out a staff member for anything they see fit, and then we all clap. In this way, time that is mandated can be molded into time well spent. Folks leave the meetings feeling energized because of the care and respect we show each other.

For the other meeting, our staff settled on a PLC-style session during which staff can choose from a bingo board of PD options or create their own. The response has been, quite frankly, game-changing. Now, instead of surviving another sit-and-get or being forced to read or do something only loosely related to our instruction or growth, we spend time on what is most important to us.

At the end of the year during summative conversations, the one common thread among staff was how they felt like they had been honored, their time had been valued, and their input had been sought and included. To me, none of it was earth-shattering, or even unique. To staff, recognizing their time as sacred marked a positive and momentous shift in our school culture.

CALL STRESS OUT BY NAME

Because it is often all-encompassing, contagious, and exhausting, stress has the power to consume us. The problem is that we often tiptoe around our personal or collective stress, in the same way we would avoid talking politics or sex on a first date. Therein lies the problem.

As leaders, we must recognize our own stress, individual teachers' stress, and the stress of our staff. Whether we are responsible for causing the stress or not, the longer we let it fester, the more likely it will derail our culture.

Call stress out by name.

As part of our yearlong exploration of #SEL4ADULTS, we enlisted the aid of a local, respected therapist, Karen Draper, who presented to our staff and PTA. Discussing everything from brain science to self-regulation techniques, Karen led our staff on a Social Emotional Learning journey for which most of us were unprepared but from which we all benefitted.

The most meaningful activity involved each of us writing our stressors on sticky notes and placing them in a brown paper bag. We could write as many or as few as we'd like as long as what we were adding to the bag was something that was actively weighing us down.

Though reluctant because of the possibility of being asked to share out, we all played along. The purpose was to illustrate how much we arrive at school with every day. Some stress can shed at the opening bell. Some stress could cause us to check our phones for updates during every quiet moment we get. Then we decided to take the activity a step further. In private or with an audience, we committed to taking our stressors out of our bag if and when we felt like we could. Of course, we all understood those same stressors could return to the bag if circumstances changed. There was real power, we decided, in calling out our stressors and taking that power back by actively removing them from our bags.

Some teachers kept their bags in their classrooms all year as a reminder of their stress and that of our students. Some teachers took them home or tucked them away in a show of protest (of the stress, not of Karen). I referred to my bag all year because I was able to take out two stressors (publishing my book and worrying about a wayward brother), though only one stayed out of my bag for good.

In the end, it didn't matter what teachers put in their bag, and I would never ask. What did matter was that I recognized our staff's collective humanity, and offered up my own, as a leadership model. I care deeply about my staff as people, not just as arbiters of our students' success. It is imperative that I illustrate this in as many creative, varied, and sometimes personal ways as possible.

IT'S PEOPLE, MAN

#SEL4ADULTS isn't a gimmick. It's not a fad. It can't be summed up in a cleverly worded tweet. It shouldn't be a one-year focus. It's not a talking point for a board of education meeting.

It's a shift in how we choose to lead.

Listen, I'm not totally naive either. I understand treating people well, caring about them, and supporting them won't necessarily lead to student success, collective empathy, or a Hollywood adaptation of our story starring Ryan Gosling (I might as well aim high, right?). But consider the alternative.

If we choose to lead by way of data points, test scores, and state-mandated self-assessments, we completely disregard the very reason we entered this profession: people.

They are people who have flaws and imperfections. People who are happy and sad at the same time. People who have growing families. People who have shrinking families. People who experience tremendous joy. People who endure unspeakable sorrow. People who can't find anything to wear. People who have something powerful to say if someone would only ask. People who prefer to listen.

When leaders choose to lead with #SEL4Adults, we honor who we once were while also creating space for who we will someday be.

∼

Brian Kulak

ABOUT THE AUTHOR

Brian Kulak is in his 21st year in education. For the first fifteen, he taught English and journalism at his alma mater in New Jersey. Working almost exclusively with seniors, Brian was committed to making connections with his students, so they could make connections with their world. He also served as a new and novice teacher mentor during which time he developed his passion for leadership. He is currently a K-5 principal in New Jersey.

In 2019, Brian published his first book, *Level Up Leadership: Advance Your EduGame*. Using the evolution of the gaming industry, the book blends gaming nostalgia, educational philosophy, and practical leadership strategies.

His blog, leveluplead.com, combines shared educational experience with his unique style. Using self-effacing humor, pop culture, and storytelling, Brian challenges readers to see themselves and their leadership differently.

His work has been featured on Edutopia, in *Educational Viewpoints*, and in *Stories in EDU*. Brian has also presented on teaching, learning, and leadership at conferences such as NJAMLE and NCTE/CEL. He's an Edcamp regular and organizer and #SEL4ADULTS advocate.

Brian is a baseball fanatic, a Pearl Jam aficionado, and a devoted family man. He lives in New Jersey with his wife and two children.

STAYING POSITIVE IN THE K-12 CLASSROOM

Deborah Kerby

I have amassed here what, hopefully, will keep you from "teacher exhaustion" and brighten your days a bit.

WHY I AM A TEACHER

My career in education did not begin in the traditional manner, high school followed by 4 to 5 years in a teacher education program. I did other types of work before I became a teacher. I worked as an accountant, a computer programmer, and a technology support consultant for many years. When my last consulting contract ended, I was looking at a very long commute if I were to remain in my field, and I did not want that lifestyle any more. I decided to pursue a career in ministry, specifically youth ministry.

God, with his ultimate sense of humor, gave me what I asked for, just not in the way I had intended. This is why prayer needs to be specific! I applied for a number of jobs in ministry and one job teaching at a K-12 alternative school. The alternative school hired me right after the interview and was my first teaching experience. Overall it was a wonderful experience, but it did not provide me with a livable wage or benefits. So, I applied to a local school district and joined the ranks of public education.

I see ministering as part of my purpose for teaching. This is not a religious thing. Ministering literally means to meet the needs of others, to take care of others, something that should be practiced in organized religion but not exclusive to it. One of the life lessons I learned is that the greatest joy comes from bringing joy to others. Ministering to others can also be a great way to pull yourself out of a funk or depression.

My first year of teaching was at a small, K-12 alternative school. The environment provided constant and varied opportunities to minister, and I realized several months in that I was ministering to staff as much as to students. It is so important for us to lift each other up. The 16 years I spent in a large public high school was similar but different from my experience in a small alternative school. In the private school everyone's issues were known by everyone; in the public school people, students and staff alike, carried layers of baggage. Attitudes and behaviors were impacted by the weight of this baggage. I worked with some people for years before I understood them. The point is that we need to be careful not to judge our students and colleagues because we don't know what they are carrying.

Through 18 years of teaching, I have made many mistakes in my teaching practice and gratefully learned from most of them. I have compiled a list of what helps me to help myself, my students, and my colleagues have a more rewarding experience in the public school environment. I hope it will help you as well.

TEACHING DO'S AND DON'TS

These **Do's and Don'ts** are written from the perspective of a K-12 classroom teacher, but many will also apply in higher education and online environments.

Don't think about how many days there are left in the school year, unless it is to inspire you to make every moment mean-

ingful. When I was teaching business classes I could never get to everything I wanted to cover in a semester, and even more so in the 45-day personal finance courses I taught. I find it is better to avoid the attitude of "let's hurry up and get out of here" and replace it with "I only have x number of days left to teach this group!" I believe that what I am teaching is important and want to make the most of the little bit of time I have each group of students.

Do start each day with an appreciation for being alive, well enough to teach, and the occasion to bring joy to others. As a teacher, you have a unique opportunity to open the hearts and minds of young people and fill them with positives.

Don't own negative things other teachers say about your student(s). You might find that a teacher's own biases influence their interpretation of who a students really is. When you get to know the student, you might find the negative was with the teacher and not with the student.

Do avoid gossip and negativity. Surround yourself with people who inspire you and lift you up. Imagine how much nicer the school would be if each day every staff member found at least one kind word to say to another.

Don't bring your personal biases and dramas to work with you. This can be difficult when you are going through trials, but it will distract you from your purpose and may bring you more difficulties in the long run.

Do remember that many in the school population, staff and student alike, have difficulties that impact their lives on a daily basis. My first five years in public school I taught across the hall from Charlie. When I I asked Charlie how he was, he ALWAYS replied, "Great!" We all know that no one is great every day, but when asked Charlie gave a positive response; he left any troubles outside of school. Charlie taught me a valuable lesson in how to greet people so that the greeting is about them and not about you. He helped me to start every school day on a positive note.

Do not ask others how they feel about something because you want to vent. This is a trap that many of us get into. Unfortunately, after the venting you may not feel any better and you have brought another person down with you. Life has shown me that most people do not want to hear your troubles unless they are looking for gossip to share with someone else.

Do be honest in your communications. If something is troubling you, it may help to share it with a trusted friend. It is not, however, beneficial to anyone for you to drag someone into your muck with you. It just makes the muck thicker and deeper. Find someone you know will just listen if all you need is to vent. Find someone who can help you affect change if that is your intention.

Don't try to keep too tight a control over your classroom. In truth, you cannot really control another person anyway. You can only control yourself and how you respond to the attitudes and behaviors of others.

Do give your students choices when possible. My experience has been that students, like everyone, enjoy having some choice in what they do. Some teachers have students write a classroom constitution each year. I have never gone to that extreme, but I allow students to make choices in how they complete assignments. When I teach a computer skill I allow students to choose the topic they use for practice if they do not want to copy word-for-word the sample I provided. I sometimes allow students to choose to work alone or with a partner. Or they may choose to present their work orally rather than in writing. Feedback from my students has consistently shown that having some choice is their favorite thing about my class.

Do not consistently reprimand students for breaking a school or classroom rule that is frequently broken. If you do, they may just tune you out. In my high school the biggest issues were district dress code and cell phone policies being broken. I believe one of the reasons these rules were a problem was because they were not uniformly enforced throughout the building; some teachers allow students to use cell phones in their class and overlook dress code violations. We all need to find a way to handle these situations that works for us. I found what worked for me which was basically a classroom policy that enforced district rules in a way students felt I respect them, and also that they had some control over the situation. Nagging, scolding, and discipline referrals only caused drama and did not have any desired outcome.

Do have clear expectations and classroom rules and consequences for your students. Be sure that your students understand your class rules and the positive and negative consequences of how well rules are followed. You cannot assume that they do. When I taught high school seniors, I showed them images of written warnings for being late to class, eating in the computer lab, and using cell phones inappropriately. I explained that this is their written warning and infractions of the rules would be dealt with according to rules outlined in the student handbook. Then I explained that I consider them to be adults and if they foresee having a problem with any of the rules that they should come to me to work it out like adults. As a result, I rarely had to consequence students for behavior. I wish someone had taught me to do this 10 years earlier than when I started, but my approach may not work for you. We all must create a classroom environment that works for us.

Don't jump to conclusions about your students' behaviors. We all have students with sick or deceased family and close friends, financial and emotional trouble at home, (Oh the drama!), and many other issues. We often are not aware of their situations, just as they are often not aware of what we are going through.

Do, always, remember that you are the adult in the room and that your students are children. They look to you for guidance and guidelines and yes, they will test you. It is in the nature of children to push until they find the lines that cannot be crossed. When those lines are clearly drawn, it makes it easier for everyone.

Do start each day fresh, with a positive attitude, and with the knowledge that what you say and do impacts those around you. Share smiles as often as you can. Listen before you speak. And always remember why teaching is so important and a wonderful experience.

When you are in a leadership role, every day you have the choice to be an agent for good, lifting up others around you and bringing a little light into darker places. Know that what you do does matter. People are always watching and learning from you.

As you begin each school year, imagine how you would like it to be at the end of the year. Imagine what you hope to achieve, to learn, to grow into. Keep this in your mind as you go through the year, and when times get tough remember that tomorrow is a new day.

ABOUT THE AUTHOR

Deborah Kerby teaches K-6 Computer Skills and Computer Science at a public school in Northeast, PA. Before teaching elementary she taught 16 years of Business and Computer classes at Pocono Mountain East High School. Deborah earned a Doctorate in Education Leadership, as well as a Certificate in Instructional Technology, from Wilkes University. Before a career in teaching she worked in Business doing Computer and Networking Support, Database Design, Programming and Accounting. She has presented on Adaptive Learning with Google Forms in a Webinar and a face-to-face session through ISTE. She also regularly contacts legislators in Harrisburg, PA and Washington, D.C. about improving education. She also regularly contacts legislators in Harrisburg, PA and Washington, D.C. about improving education.

RE-INVENTING YOURSELF AFTER EXPERIENCING TEACHER BURNOUT

Dr. Marquita S. Blades

There is more than one way to be an educator.

After 16 years, six schools, 10 classrooms, four school districts and one charter school, five grade levels, and nine principals, I found myself resigning from the professional I'd pursued since childhood. Up until that point, teaching had been my entire world. Although I had dabbled in other things in order to supplement my income, I had every intention of completing a full 30 years in the classroom. I was not interested in becoming a principal. At most, I saw myself advancing to an Instructional Coach or Curriculum Director, but whatever leadership position I sought, it would be directly linked to classroom instruction – something connected to the primary duties and responsibilities of a teacher.

Three weeks into my 17th year in the classroom, I decided to take a medical leave, which would ultimately lead to my resignation. It was not an easy decision to make. It was necessary, but it was not easy. Who walks away from the career that they enjoy? At that point in time, I had gotten my second wind in education. After facing burning and getting over the hump, I was working in a school that I loved, teaching my favorite subject, and was poised for advancement in the profession. So again, I ask, who walks away from a career that they enjoy? Especially during a time when they are thriving?

Until recently, the phenomenon of Teacher Burnout has not received the amount of attention it deserves. I can admit that I didn't fully understand it myself until after I had gotten past it. I'd blamed the time period of my discontent with teaching strictly on the health issues that I had experienced, but after deep reflection, I realized there was a combination of issues that led to being dissatisfied with teaching. Things like bullying from administrators, lack of support from parents, disrespectful students, and unreasonable working conditions. For a long time, I told myself that this was just "how it is" in education and that if I loved the profession, I'd just have to deal with it.

At the point that I resigned, I had fallen back in love with teaching, but I could no longer handle the physical demands of consistently performing well in the classroom. I couldn't stand the thought of no longer teaching, but I also knew I could not give my students the best of me. It was time for me to do education in a different way.

Throughout my years teaching, I'd spent my summers planning and managing national summer programs for high school students. This involved me serving as what would be equivalent to a project manager, curriculum director, and school administrator all rolled into one. My summers consisted of me recruiting, hiring and training staff, managing the day-to-day program logistics, booking speakers and planning site visits. All skills that could easily be transferred into a business of my own. An education consulting business.

Just like that, I became an education consultant! I took the best of the best of my classroom teaching experience and program management experience and developed workshops that I felt could benefit teachers. I am making it sound a lot easier than it was, but in a nutshell, I simply became a consultant. Of course, there were doubts. Is my content valuable? How will I get clients? How much should I charge? Heck, *who* was going to pay me for any of this?

Even though I knew I was a great teacher with excellent strategies, I'd never been Teacher of the Year, so I didn't know if anyone else would find merit in what I had to say. I'd applied for several leadership positions within the school districts I'd worked for and never so much as got an interview. I could not boast of ever having the highest test scores. I hadn't networked with the right people and I wasn't outgoing. How in the world was I going to back up this new title I'd blessed myself with? All I knew for sure was that I was not done with education and it was not done with me. After connecting with mentors, learning how to run a business, and paying dues on the speaking circuit, I was able to carve a niche for myself and create a name that is now recognized and respected by many of the nation's most popular and successful educators.

Sometimes, we have to find a different way to get there. Teaching in the classroom is not right for every teacher. Working in the public school system in just one way to impact students. As educators, we have to stop self-sacrificing and learn how our talents will best benefit the profession and ultimately students. It is okay to get tired of being in the classroom and want more. It's okay to admit that being in the classroom is too much at times. Some people can weather the storm and others will need to find shelter and re-invent themselves.

What are the options for teachers who feel that the traditional classroom setting has run its course? Let's see, there's developing and managing summer and after-school programs, teaching online, curriculum writing, policy and advocacy work, and educational nonprofits. Dare I suggest opening your own independent school? The key is taking the time to reflect on your natural talents and abilities along with your most effective strategies employed as an educator. Build your practice around those things.

Sometimes burnout is only for a season, sometimes it is indicative of something more. Sometimes it is the signal that it is time to reinvent yourself as an educator. What's most important is that you are doing what you love and are passionate about in a way that students can receive the very best that you have to offer.

Dr. Marquita S. Blades

ABOUT THE AUTHOR

Dr. Marquita S. Blades is an award-winning STEM Educator and Teacher EmPOWARRment Specialist with 16 years of experience as a high school science teacher and manager of national STEM programs. Dr. Blades is currently a full-time Education Consultant, the owner of Dr. Blades Consulting, LLC which offers solutions to learning institutions and organizations through professional development programs, curriculum and assessment writing, conference programming, and individual teacher/education consultant coaching services.

Dr. Marquita S. Blades saves schools and school districts time and money by teaching them to increase student engagement & collaboration through rigorous and meaningful learning experiences, using the resources they currently have on-hand. Her areas of specialty workshops include: Practical Implementation of the Next Generation Science Standards and POWARRful Teaching Strategies for Increasing Student Engagement.

Shortly after resigning from teaching full-time, Dr. Blades created The Mediocre Teacher Project, which helps other teachers avoid and battle through burnout by incorporating their unique gifts and talents into their daily practice. In 2016, Dr. Blades launched The Dr. Marquita Blades Show-Candid Conversations that Create Change, a radio show dedicated to discussing current trends and issues in education. Dr. Blades is a contributing author for *The Whole Truth Anthology* which was released in 2017, the lead author for Amazon best-selling anthology, *The Mediocre Teacher Project*, and just recently completed her first book of instructional strategies entitled: *POWARRful Teaching Strategies for Increasing Engagement & Collaboration While Maintaining Rigor in Science Courses*.

Dr. Blades is also a Co-Founder of the Gyrlfriend Collective, a full-service, independent publishing house responsible for the best-selling Gyrlfriend Code™ Anthology series (www.gyrlfriendcollective.com). Gyrlfriend Collective is devoted to collaborating with women, offering social support, and opportunities for professional development through publishing and coaching programs.

Dr. Blades is a member of Sigma Gamma Rho Sorority, Inc. and The National Sorority of Phi Delta Kappa. She has received numerous awards including the Elizabeth Allen Alford Overcomer's Award (2017), Teachers of Atlanta Honoree (2017), Eta Sigma Chapter of Sigma Gamma Rho Sorority, Inc. Rising Star in Education (2017), National Celebrity Educators™-Georgia Celebrity Educator of the Year (2018), and Women of Strength Honoree (2018). Most recently, she was nominated for the 2019 Community Engagement R.I.C.E. Award and was selected to be included in the 2019 Edition of Who's Who in Black Atlanta.

Dr. Blades holds a BIS in Broad Field Science from Georgia State University, an MS in Technical and Professional Communication from Southern Polytechnic State University, and an Ed.D. in Instructional Leadership from Nova Southeastern University. Dr. Blades enjoys reading, cooking, and traveling with her husband. Learn more about Dr. Blades by visiting www.drmarquitablades.com.

#SELFCARE IS NOT JUST A HASHTAG

Dyann Wilson

> We need to learn to love ourselves first, in all our glory and our imperfections.
>
> — JOHN LENNON

Selfcare is not just a hashtag. When reading that I instantly think, "Well, I am guilty of this." We all see them on social media; cute quotes for educators and then this..#SelfCare. Burnout does not discriminate and it reaches more than just educators. Burnout can be silent and it can be loud. We simply cannot post quotes and not live it ourselves. Burnout is everywhere in education. We see it more prevalent on social media where educators get a chance to vent. When it comes to burnout, we have to be more proactive with our self-care. Healthy dialogue is what we desperately need.

A BAD DAY IS NOT A BAD LIFE!!

Recently my twin sister Amy Storer "fell," as she put it on her Twitter post. She stated that she sat on that "thorn" for a while. She spent so much time beating herself up that she lost focus on the lesson to be learned. GROWTH as an educator means not giving up when feeling defeated; it is persevering and remembering your WHY.

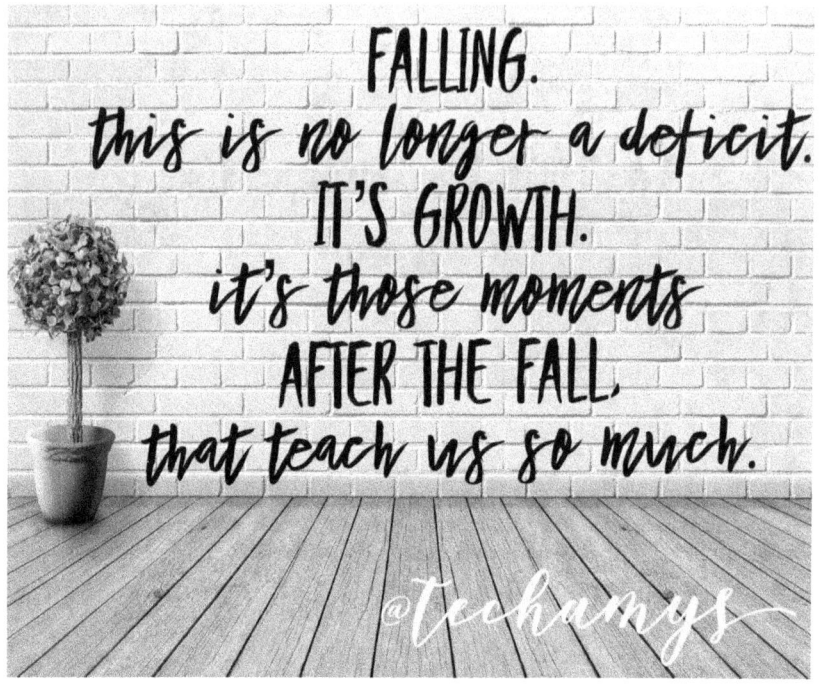

The question becomes, "In order for me to truly learn, do I need to fall?"

"Teacher burnout is almost epidemic in this country and is one of the causes of the 17 percent annual attrition rate among educators. Scientists have found that teachers can burnout from the negative emotions and inefficacy they feel around the challenges of managing their students" (Zakrzewski, 2012).

Let's get real for a moment. Too many times people say to take care of you and yours or you cannot be enough for your students. But is that enough? I believed that at one point and even lived like that, but I continually was stressed over things I could not control. Those stressors would manifest into different reactions. It was like a cycle with no end. I would come home and vent to my husband, which is healthy, but

I relived those stressors all over again questioning if I handled them correctly. But what I have learned through all my years in education is GRACE—not only to myself but to others. Giving myself permission to extend compassion to myself and even self-kindness. Kristin Neff is the author of Self Compassion and in this book, she makes some amazing statements that have stuck with me. "Neff has found that people who practice self-compassion experience fewer negative emotions and stay emotionally balanced in a difficult situation--both of which, according to a study on emotional exhaustion among teachers, help prevent teacher burnout" (Zakrzewski, 2012).

We should all treat ourselves with the same care we show others. As a school counselor, I deal with empathy and self-compassion daily. Instead of feeling your student's pain we should be embracing our students' pain. Make these moments teachable not only to your students but to yourself. But do I show that to myself daily?

The counseling team I am a part of is my crew. It is almost like a teacher forum but these ladies are some of my closest friends and confidants. We vent to each other, laugh with each other, cry with each other, and by doing this we are self-caring. This has helped me tremendously with my mindset and mindfulness. I am surrounded by people who practice mindfulness and also are a positivity of light around other staff members and students. I cannot stress enough how important it is to have a strong peer network.

There is so much power in practicing self-care in front of students too. Students pick up on so many things and we want them to ultimately see that by practicing self-compassion they can deal with challenges in a healthy way. It can become a ripple effect on your campus.

Lastly I want to speak on advocating for yourselves and others in regards to self-care on your campus. Go to your administrators and school leaders and ask that professional development be offered that are centered around self-care and/or mindfulness. There should always be a safe place for educators to go and talk to someone. Whether it be inviting a counselor or using your own counselors to utilize PD to train your educators on healthy coping skills, mindfulness, and self-care.

In closing, I want to end with a cluster of sentences that has been stamped on this little counselor's heart forever.

> You cannot eradicate or prevent all suffering for your students. But you can show up each day, support your students, advocate for them, and love them. Begin each morning by thinking of your students and say to yourself: I will provide a loving and safe environment in my classroom today. At the end of each day, breathe in slowly to calm your system. Breathe out and say I have done good work today. I will let the stress and worry go until tomorrow.
>
> — GUNN, 2018

REFERENCES

Gunn, J. (2018, June 22). Self Care for Teachers Who Educate Traumatized Students. Retrieved from https://education.cu-portland.edu/blog/classroom-resources/self-care-for-teachers/

Zakrzewski, V. (2012, September 11). How Self-Compassion Can Help Prevent Teacher Burnout. Retrieved from https://greatergood.berkeley.edu/article/item/self_compassion_for_teac

Dyann Wilson

ABOUT THE AUTHOR

Dyann Wilson is a school counselor at Teague Middle within Aldine ISD. Dyann has been in education for over 13 years and this will be her fifth year as a counselor. She is also an ambassador for Texas On Course which supports College and Career Readiness. Her passion is advocating for her profession and students. Dyann believes it is so important to be a lifelong learner and to truly get involved and network. Her students are her teachers and she is constantly learning how to be a better counselor through her experiences with them. She hopes that through this process she will be able to network with others and to learn new things. Dyann is married to the most amazing man, Charles Wilson, and they have three beautiful children, Bre, Nancy, and Finn. She loves to camp, kayak, go to beaches, eat amazing food, travel, work out, and just live life to the fullest. Most importantly is that she does these things with her family...SELF CARE.

TEACHER SELF-CARE: WHY IT IS NECESSARY

Raye Wood, NBCT, Ed.D.

Find ways to take care of yourself as a teacher so you can be the best you can be in your classroom.

Teachers arguably have the most important jobs in the world: we allow every other profession to be possible. However, along with the importance of our work, we also have one of the most stressful jobs. We are constantly bombarded with new mandates, a lack of effective curriculum materials and an evaluation system that may make teaching competitive rather than collaborative. It should not surprise anyone that we continue to see a staggering 44% of our teaching force voluntarily quit the profession within their first five years in the classroom (Will, 2018).

The real question is: what can we do about this? Unfortunately, we cannot control what happens in the legislature and often teachers have little to no say in how things are done locally in their own schools and districts. It is important to realize that we can only control what we do. Yes, absolutely stand up, protest, write to your representatives and whatever else you need to do in order to have your voice heard. What I really want you to do, however, is something you can do immediately: engage in teacher self-care.

MY TEACHING STORY

When I was a brand-new teacher, I was so excited to get into my first classroom and make a difference for my students. I was not hired until after Thanksgiving and I was replacing a teacher who had left that classroom a gigantic mess. I threw myself into that long-term sub job as a way to prove myself and hoped it would lead to a full-time position of my own. Fortunately, my tenacity paid off and I was hired into a full contract the following school year.

Unfortunately, the precedent had been set. I thought I had to work really hard and always go above and beyond in order to keep proving myself. I rarely said no when asked to take on additional roles or responsibilities and I found myself on so many committees and teams that I was out of my classroom at least once per week for some meeting or other. It was chaotic and stressful and certainly wasn't in the best interest of me or my family (or my students!).

I changed schools in the fall of 2010 thinking that would help, but it did not. I continued to go above and beyond and push myself to the highest limits. Even looking back now, I'm not sure what I was trying to prove, but I do know that my efforts and tenacity were appreciated by no one. Let me repeat that: *my efforts were appreciated by <u>no one</u>*. That's the rub of it, of course, when you finally recognize that you've been working yourself to the bone and no one actually cares or appreciates that you've sacrificed so much personally.

This came to a head in the 2016-2017 school year when I was the testing coordinator at my school. The reality was that the principal was supposed to do the hard work and the teacher representative was supposed to support the principal, but that's not how it worked. We had a brand new principal who didn't know what she was doing and thus she put all of the coordinator responsibilities on me. Keep in mind I was also teaching a full-time elementary classroom. I didn't complain about it, I just made it happen so that things would go smoothly for everyone during the stressful testing season. We were sitting in a staff meeting and I made a comment about how I needed folks to work with me on the testing and provide whatever information if I asked for it so there wouldn't be bumps in the road. One of my colleagues said she felt like I really needed to be thanked for everything I was doing because if I was asking for help it meant I was overwhelmed. It was only at that point that my principal thanked me for doing all of the testing, but it wasn't heart-felt. She literally looked at me, half-shrugged and said, "Yeah, thanks."

Needless to say, I didn't stick around that school for the following year. But I also didn't really learn my lesson either. I still was not good at saying no, I still took on way too many responsibilities and didn't push back enough when I did try to ask for grace and admit I was overwhelmed and needed to back off a little.

It wasn't until the 2018-2019 school year when things really compounded. I was overwhelmed, knew all of the extra responsibilities I had taken on were not being appreciated and I was *tired*. Just flat out tired of trying to do it all and knowing full well that if I stopped doing the things I was doing, no one would probably even notice. Therefore, putting myself into the grave over these frivolous responsibilities just was not worth it. I had no choice but to step back, begin some real self-care and put myself and my family above my job.

SELF-CARE: WHAT IS IT?

According to HealthPrep (2019), self-care describes "any activity that individuals undertake deliberately to help with their physical, emotional and mental health." Self-care can be any activity that a person enjoys that reduces anxiety, releases stress and helps to improve someone's overall mood.

Just as every person is unique and has different interests and tastes, self-care will look different for every person who engages with it. For someone who is more introverted, self-care might include taking a walk or hike in a secluded area where they can be alone and connect with nature, reading a book, or binge-watching a favorite television program on a Saturday afternoon with their favorite blanket and a cup of coffee. For someone who is more extroverted and enjoys being around people, self-care might include going out to lunch with friends, having a manicure/pedicure or enjoying a kid-free date with their partner.

Self-care can include physical, mental and emotional activities. It does not matter what activities you choose as long as you do something to deliberately unwind and take care of yourself. Physical activities can include exercise, sports or even massages and bubble baths. Mental and emotional self-care is a little more abstract and can be harder for people to pinpoint what it is. Acknowledging emotions without judgement is good self-care; allow yourself to feel sad, angry, hurt, or whatever other emotions you have without feeling guilty about having them. Using positive self-talk and acknowledging your struggles can also be a good way to engage with mental self-care.

SELF-CARE: WHY IS IT IMPORTANT?

The number one reason self-care is so important for teachers is because we are in a giving profession. We constantly give our all to our students and the other adults we work with so that they can be productive and happy. If we do not engage in self-care, however, we will not be as effective at our jobs, in being parents, loved ones, or just good people in general.

Think of a time when you stayed up way too late. You may have been finishing a personal project, meeting a work deadline or were up and down all night with a sick child or spouse. You didn't want to take a sick day so you went to work despite feeling like you were dragging your heels. How did you fare at work that day? Were you at the top of your game? Probably not. You may have lost your temper over something that didn't really matter or forgotten to do something that really needed to be done because your brain was not processing as well because you were tired.

If this happens to you often and you are not engaging in self-care strategies, it can be a recipe for disaster.

MY TEACHING STORY REVISITED

I spent more than 10 years as a classroom teacher without really taking care of myself. Self-care and I were not friends. We were not even acquaintances. I am guilty of constantly saying yes to everyone else's demands and ignoring my own needs. (If I'm being really honest, I also ignored the needs of my family because there is always an opportunity cost; if you say yes at work for something outside of school hours, no matter what it is for, you are saying no to something that you could do with your family or for yourself.)

Despite making school changes in the fall of 2010 and the fall of 2017, I still hadn't really learned my lesson. I wasn't really taking care of myself, I wasn't saying no nearly often enough and I was really struggling to try to be the Superwoman other people apparently thought I was. I had way too many responsibilities and I still wasn't really engaging in self-care the way I should have been.

In November 2018, after some big changes at work, including a mid-year transition to a split grade classroom with the largest class size in the school, I reached a boiling point. I was unhappy and miserable. It affected me personally and it affected my husband and kids. It obviously affected me at work too but I was so good at hiding it, most people didn't even know anything was not okay. The experience made me so much more aware of why self-care is so incredibly important.

Even if you don't have a story that is similar to mine, self-care is vital. I would argue it is especially important and vital for those of us in careers like teaching where so much of our hearts are put out into the world in the service of others. We cannot effectively take care of other people if we are not taking care of ourselves.

I know this to be true. Once I finally learned to put myself first and take back control, I found I was and am happier and healthier. I also know that I will be better in my classroom if I am not constantly overworked and can focus on things I care about but things I also get pleasure from.

SELF-CARE EXAMPLES & IDEAS

There are so many different ways you can engage in self-care. It really is up to you, but remember that true self-care is engaging in something that brings positive energy and balance back to you. If something makes you feel anxious or nervous, it would not count as self-care. Here are some examples and ideas you can try.

Say No - If something truly is not going to benefit you and be time well spent, say no to it. This is a hard lesson I still grapple with at times. Teachers are used to sacrificing themselves for the sake of the greater good, however, it is absolutely okay and necessary to really examine the commitment you are being asked to be part of. If it is a one-and-done type of event, there is probably no harm in saying yes if you want to do so. But something that is going to take considerable time and energy that just doesn't excite you? It is okay to take care of yourself and say no to those types of requests.

Journaling - Writing in a journal is an excellent way to engage in self-care. The best news is, you can also make the journal whatever you want. It can be a doodle journal, a bullet journal, a gratitude journal, a mindfulness journal or any other type of journal you want to use.

I have utilized a combination of a mindfulness journal and a gratitude journal to help me engage in self-care. Each morning I would set an intention for the day and state what I would be mindful of (and often that would be things like "I will be mindful of my negative self talk" so that if I caught myself being negative, I could easily switch to positive talk instead). At the end of each day, I would complete the gratitude portion and state something I was grateful for. By taking time each day to focus myself by setting an intention in the morning and reflecting each afternoon, I was able to really take time to think about myself and where I was in my own head each day.

Meditation - Spending time meditating can help you spend time in your own head in a positive way. Apps like *Calm* and *Insight Timer* have free options where you can complete guided meditations that help you to learn to notice your thoughts and let them drift away without judging them or yourself.

I personally found meditation to be a little weird when I first tried it out. After a week or so, however, I came to really look forward to that ten-minute daily time that was reserved just for me. I put my earbuds in, closed my eyes and lost myself in the soothing tones and background sounds. I learned to clear my head and focus on the present moment. It is a cherished ritual I like to engage with in the morning before I get my day started.

Did you know that as a full-time educator, you can get the premium version of *Calm* for free? Visit calm.com/schools to sign up. (You must have a valid school email address.)

Therapy - Therapy might seem like a strange thing to put on a list of things you can do to engage in self-care, but I think for some people this might be a good way to take out some time for yourself. Especially if you struggle with mental health issues, talking to a therapist can be really helpful. It provides you with a safe space to share concerns, insecurities, and focus on a plan for empowering yourself. It can be a bit odd to share your deepest insecurities with someone you don't know, but having a trained and licensed listener can help you to make a plan while also providing you with someone who will help keep you accountable for sticking to your plan.

I have engaged with two different therapists. One was in person therapy where I visited her office once a week. Currently I utilize TalkSpace to work with a licensed therapist. Having the flexibility to check in each day rather than waiting to unload everything once a week is really helpful for me and the lifestyle that I lead. There is no one-size-fits-all model for therapy, but it can be an incredibly beneficial practice to help you engage in self-care.

Walking/Bike Riding - Communing with nature can be a wonderful way to take care of yourself. If you live somewhere with walking or biking trails, you can enjoy the great outdoors while also doing something that is good for you. If you desire, you can even have a friend or two join you on these excursions and talk while you're walking or biking.

Reading - Reading for fun can also be a good way to engage in self-care. You can get lost in someone else's world and forget about your own for a while.

Exercising - Aside from walking or bike riding, taking up an exercise class or joining a gym can be a great way to take care of yourself too. I know I enjoy putting in my earbuds and just giving it my all on whatever machine I chose that day. It can be a great way to relieve stress and it's good for you.

Pampering - Simply taking care of your physical self through pampering can be a great form of self-care. Take a luxurious bubble bath, have your nails done, get a haircut, hang out in the man cave if that's what recharges you. Do something that makes you feel cherished and well cared for.

There is no right or wrong way to engage with self-care. As long as the activities you choose help you to relax, unwind and relieve stress, they count. (Of course, be safe and responsible in your choices too.) You will feel better and find you have so much more presence to bring to your daily tasks because you are giving yourself time to exist and enjoy life on your own terms. You are using your nurture side to care for yourself so that you are more able to care for others as time goes on.

REFERENCES

Healthprep. (2019). Beginner's guide to self-care for mental health. *HealthPrep*. Retrieved from: **https://tinyurl.com/yxhcnna4**

Will, M. (2018). 5 things to know about today's teaching force. *Education Week*. Retrieved from: **https://tinyurl.com/y3zcglc7**

Raye Wood, NBCT, Ed.D.

ABOUT THE AUTHOR

Raye Wood is a K-8 ESL Teacher in Michigan. She has taught for 13 years in grades 2-5. She holds a Master's degree in Teaching English to Speakers of Other Languages (TESOL), National Board Certification in Early/Middle Childhood LIteracy and a Doctor of Education in Teacher Leadership. She is passionate about Restorative Practices and teacher voice. With a clinical diagnosis of depression and anxiety, Raye understands how important self care is for everyone but especially those who work in service industries where so much of their job including caring for and supporting others.

PART FIVE: ALL HANDS ON DECK

BLACK PARENTS MUST BE ENGAGED IN SCHOOL TURNAROUND WORK

Jason B. Allen

Black parents must be married to their child's education Pre-K through 12th grade.

It never fails. Each school year we start strong with family engagement only to be left asking this question later, where are the parents?

As an inner-city teacher, each school year we get excited about welcoming our new families. However, it's hard to avoid the realization that it will be the last time we see or hear from the majority of the parents. Unfortunately, many schools struggle with keeping parents engaged. Especially in schools that aren't serving Black and Brown students well academically.

I've been doing the work of family and community engagement for over six years across Metro Atlanta. I can tell you that parents are present. They are working, they are contributing, raising and supporting their families. But Black children have been disenfranchised in American schools for decades. So many school districts are doing school turnaround efforts to help change the disproportionate number of Black students, especially Black boys, who are being left behind in schools.

There are a lot of variables that lead to the lack of parental presence in many struggling and low-performing schools. Of course, many parents simply have work schedules that conflict with school events and meetings. Some parents may be only slightly older than teenagers themselves, and many parents are also products of failing schools and have never seen examples of what productive relationships between schools and families can look like. All of these factors may contribute to the absence of parents from school.

Take a moment and think from the perspective of the families at your school. Does your school feel truly welcoming? It's time to lift up our "students," not label them! Imagine if our Georgia students weren't labeled by standardized tests. We must acknowledge that all of our students aren't being labeled, and who exactly is. For some Georgia parents, they can't begin to imagine what success looks like when survival is the only option for their child.

What we learned from the Atlanta cheating scandal is that high stakes tests put unnecessary pressure on school leaders, teachers, and students. As a former APS employee of 12 years, I've seen first hand the damage this has on Black and Brown boys in lower income communities.

Black boys have been stereotyped for years in schools through data produced by standardized tests. I remember the pressure and stigma placed on Black boys for not being able to excel on these tests. I remember teachers during my time in school and in schools where I have worked making statements around how Black boys can add but they can't read.

Educational advocates have brought a lot of awareness to the school to prison pipeline and how private prisons use standardized test data for Black boys as early as third grade to determine how many beds to make for prisons based off if they pass now. Discipline impacts how standardized tests are designed and implemented. As a result, children of color, often Black boys who rank highest in school discipline data and suspensions are impacted heavily. I mean talk about the pressure on Black boys in schools who are targets of being sentenced to prison if they don't pass the "test" in third grade.

We have to be more intentional about supporting, empowering and including parents in the decisions regarding their child's education.

HOW CAN SCHOOLS SUCCESSFULLY ENGAGE BLACK PARENTS?

1. Build real relationships.

It starts with building relationships! School leaders and educators have to be intentional about engaging parents and families.

2. Start early.

Reinforcing support and resources for more early learning centers in areas of at-risk and failing schools.

3. Share tools for teaching and learning.

Building effective academic support programs for parents to continue education at home.

It's important to remember that families are a child's first source of education. They learn language, conflict resolution, how to treat others, and most importantly how to respect and love themselves from the adults around them before they even enter school.

4. Establish clear expectations.

In order to maintain a strong partnership with parents, schools must have clear expectations and processes to hold parents accountable and vice versa. Accountability best serves the organization and parents when there are clear expectations of them.

5. Fight for equity.

We have to be change agents in and out of the classroom. Social injustices contribute to the presence of failing and underperforming schools.

School turnaround cannot be done without parents. Strategies provides to parents from schools should include engaging ways to excel learning at home. If parents aren't excited about learning then school turnaround work won't be as impactful for the students who need it most.

It's hard to imagine equity in education for Black boys in the State of Georgia when they are constantly placed into a subgroup and labeled as low performing. I hear statements like this often from Black parents regarding their sons' educational experiences and the impact standardized testing has had on them.Standardized tests have been used to categorize, separate, discriminate and create bad cultures for schools.

Parents have to be empowered to hold their school leaders, community leaders, elected officials and even other parent leaders within the community accountable. It takes a village to raise a child—that's all of us—but we have to know the role that we play and why it's important to the success of our children.

Jason B. Allen

ABOUT THE AUTHOR

Jason B. Allen has worked in Education for over fifteen (15) years as a teacher and leader servicing students, families and communities. He began as an ELA teacher and most recently served in school administration. He saw the disproportionate numbers of Black boys in Special Education, being suspended or expelled from school and decided to go back to the classroom as a Special Education teacher to make a bigger impact.

Throughout his career, he has mentored Black boys through his national mentoring program, BMWI (Black Men with Initiative). As an education advocate and blogger, Jason actively speaks and writes on ways to improve educating Black boys and building Black Male Engagement in schools.

His passion for community service led him to become an advocate for family and community engagement, special education and Black boys. He recently finished the Family & Community Engagement Program at Harvard led by Dr. Karen Mapp. As a blogger for the Education Post, he uses his platform on EdLanta to raise awareness of ways to improve how we educate Black boys as well as recruiting Black Male Educators.

Jason leads his family's non-profit organization, Lillie's Foundation, that supports grandparents raising school aged children and is currently the Board Chair of the State of Georgia's first charter commissioned school for all girls. Embedding the spirit of service, the main goal of Mr. Allen is to simply help others along his life's journey. He's dedicated to servicing those in need, determined to do the right thing for the right reasons to ensure the advancement of Black boys in our community schools.

SHOULD YOU HIRE A TECH COACH ... OR A TECH CONDUCTOR?

Jeffrey D. Bradbury

Before your school hires your next Instructional Specialist, take a step back and think about what should be qualifications for the task at hand.

The other day, I had a technology coach from a neighboring school district visit my school and shadow me for the day. It was a fantastic experience and something that I hope to be able to do with other districts this year and beyond. The teacher and I had a great day of learning from one another, but I couldn't help but use the day to reflect on many of our common conversation topics. One of the deep conversations we had was around the simple question: "What is a Tech Coach?"

Rather than use this post as an opportunity to dive into what a Tech Coach is, and what a Technology Integration Specialist is, I would like to propose a question to my readers that might shed some light on how I have approached these titles and my current position for the last two years. The question is one that might sound strange, but those knowing my background might find quite interesting. Should I consider myself a Tech Coach ... or a Tech Conductor?

Let's dive into this topic!

EVERYTHING I KNOW...I LEARNED FROM THE PODIUM

It's no secret that my background is in Music Education. I have countless memories of rehearsal sessions and amazing performances of the world's greatest pieces of music. About 10 years ago (or more) I decided that I wanted to get up and instead of sitting in the orchestra, I wanted to start down a path that allowed me to stand in front of the orchestra and work alongside them to perform sonata's, symphonies, and operas.

It was during that time that I started taking formal conducting lessons from several amazing teachers. From there, I learned how to physically stand and present myself to not only an orchestra, but a paying audience, and of course work alongside a board of directors to help promote my vision, the orchestra's vision, and most importantly, the composer's visions.

OF ALL THE THINGS THAT I LEARNED IN THE WORLD OF CONDUCTING, THESE LESSONS STAND OUT:

- The conductor is the only one on stage that doesn't make noise, yet his actions are what tie the group together.
- The musicians don't need a conductor to know what to do. A conductor's job is simply to start everyone and guide them through transitions.
- Treat every musician with respect, but understand that different instruments require different needs.

It has been through these lessons that I approach every day as a Tech Coach. It is through these lessons that I find myself becoming a Tech Conductor. Let me try and explain how these lessons can be applied in a school system.

FROM PODIUM TO CLASSROOM ... AND BACK AGAIN

When you break down everything that happens on the podium, it starts and stops with the simple concept of Respect. I can honestly say that I have my good days and I have had my bad days as I learn how to be a Tech Coach to over 400 staff members. As a conductor, you have your good days and bad days too. You have your rehearsals where everything goes well, and you have those times where someone puts you on the spot in a rehearsal and you simply don't know the answer. This happens in the classroom all the time.

What is important is that you come prepared to every rehearsal, meeting, and classroom as prepared as possible. If you don't know the answer to a question, you always make sure you have a resource (your PLN) that can help you find the answer quickly.

From early on in my conductor training, I learned that the word Maestro is one that gets placed upon you from day one, but the concept of Maestro, a word that literally translates into Teacher, (or coach) is one that is earned day after day, rehearsal after rehearsal and is earned only through respect. This is extremely true for Technology Coaches who not only work with everyone in a district at all levels but must also be walking talking resource centers of technology and pedagogy that are essentially on call 24/7.

YOU ARE THE ONLY ONE WHO DOESN'T MAKE ANY SOUND

In an orchestra setting, the violin players, play the violin, the tuba players play the tuba, and the bass players play the bass. Each of these musicians or groups of musicians has an instrument that they can pick up anytime and practice. A conductor, on the other hand, has the orchestra. There is no try way to practice late at night with an imaginary group of 50 people. The preparation for conductors is mostly mental and requires you to study scores of music and practice "gestures" in the air, sometimes in front of mirrors to make sure that the one single time you are in front of a group you get it right.

As a Tech Coach, it is very much the same. Teachers have the opportunity to learn from their students every day. They learn how their classrooms work, act, and interact with each other. As a Tech Coach, you have just one moment to walk into a classroom and nail your lesson. When you are given an opportunity to present in front of a building, you are given an opportunity to showcase yourself in front of 150 (or more) strangers who are all there to learn from and support you. They know you are in front of them to help them become better educators, but there might not be the same friendly connection that a teacher and a group of students has, or a principal and a faculty have.

Walking into a building to give PD is very much like being asked to come into a new orchestra and guest conduct a rehearsal or performance without ever getting to meet the musicians.

YOUR TEACHERS…THEY DON'T NEED YOU

Let's face the fact that teachers have been teaching for hundreds of years without the need for a "Technology Integration Specialist." They don't need "Tech Coaching." But … do they?

One of the first rules of conducting is *show up when needed and get out of the way.*

There are times when you can simply tell a musician how to play something, times when you can describe a sound, and times where you have to grab an instrument from the violin section and demonstrate for a group.

This couldn't be truer as a Tech Coach. There are times where I have worked with a teacher and my role was simply to answer a question or two and back away. Other situations lead me to help them create a co-teaching lesson where together, we worked with the students on an innovative lesson.

In the classroom, the role of a Tech Coach is to quickly enter and assess a situation and provide whatever the teacher needs when they need it. Perhaps it's by simply answering a question and other times it's by picking up the instrument to demonstrate how something should look or sound.

If you choose the right method of support, the group/teacher will appreciate your help and together the rehearsal/lesson will move forward. If you choose the wrong method at the wrong time, you are liable to insult someone and create a situation you never intended to have started. As a Conductor and as a Tech Coach, it's always important to know the personalities you are working with so you can quickly make the right decisions and choices.

SOME TEACHERS ARE SECTION PLAYERS ... SOME ARE SOLOISTS

If you really think about it, a school district is very much like an orchestra. To conceptualize this, let's break down the different parts of each.

The Orchestra

The Strings

In the front of a symphony orchestra lies a massive section known as the Strings. Altogether, their instruments are in the "violin family." Their instruments look similar, they play with a bow, and there could be as many as 24 of the same instrument in each of the 5 distinct sections. Together, they can be broken down into string quartets, trios, and often, composers write for them as either a full section or as soli sections. Each of the subsections (violins, viola, cello, bass) are seated by rank (ability level) and there is a section leader who is for conversation's sake, "the boss" of that section.

The Winds

The next group of musicians behind the strings is the Woodwinds. This section is composed of your Flutes, Oboes, Clarinets, and Bassoons. They are your mid-range, mid-level instruments who are put in the awkward position of sitting behind the massive string section, yet they sit in front of the might brass and percussion sections so it's often possible that while playing loud and proud they don't get heard when the entire group is playing together.

The Brass, Percussion, Etc.

Composed of the Trumpets, Trombones, and Tubas, Drums, Marimbas, Cymbals, and all other instruments these musicians are highly specialized and are only in your group because, like the winds, they passed an audition based on their ability to be leaders and soloists. When addressing these musicians a conductor should simply be able to describe in as few words as possible the sound or quality they wish to hear and it should happen with as little retakes as possible. These are HIGHLY skilled and trained musicians who spend hours in a practice room learning what is known as "excerpts" or very tiny solo passages just to have the opportunity to audition for the group.

A School District

Elementary Teachers

Elementary teachers should be approached as a you would approach a string section—as a group. In any building, for example, you have several fourth-grade teachers all teaching their own class, but teaching a common curriculum to the classroom next door. They meet in departments to plan common activities but they often do their lesson plans on their own. When you work with one and not the others, it is often not looked highly on. Sometimes it's best to talk about concepts such as blended learning, or SAMR models, but they are also the first to allow a Tech Coach to pick up their instrument (classroom) and come in to demonstrate something new and amazing in the world of Technology.

Elementary teachers often have degrees in general elementary education rather than a specialized degree in a subject area and for that reason, it's often best to show a wide variety of examples and build lessons together. Elementary Teachers and Buildings should be approached the same way a string section is approached. It's always best when you are able to demonstrate the concept as well as described.

Middle School

Much like the proud woodwinds, middle school teachers are caught between elementary and high school teachers. They have the hardest job because without them, students don't have a solid direction when they get into the older grades. Also much like the Woodwinds, Middle School teachers are soloists who often times are remembered the most when a student looks back at their favorite years in school Their hardest job is that they often have to work with a group of students who came from multiple elementary schools oftentimes and haven't yet gelled together as individuals yet…and oh, did we mention those wonderful puberty years?

High School

Much like a conductor should never (unless specialized themselves in the instrument) tell a brass player how to play the trumpet, a good Tech Coach should never (or hardly ever) approach a high school teacher and tell them how to teach their subject—trust me…

High school teachers are HIGHLY talented, and HIGHLY specialized educators (much like the brass or woodwind soloists) who command the respect of teenagers every day and for those reasons I love popping my head into classrooms each day, asking if they need anything and moving on. Often, I find myself sitting down with high school teachers to plan out lessons the same way I would sit down with a soloist to plan out a solo passage in a symphony. If you show them respect, they will reciprocate and come back time and time again because their only goal each year is to produce the best students and pass them on to college.

TECH COACHING OR CONDUCTING … WHAT DO YOU THINK?

As I move deeper and deeper into the world of tech coaching, I often think back to the lessons I learned on the podium and try to modify them to my new surroundings. I am curious to learn what your thoughts are on the position or the roles and responsibilities of your current situation.

For more information about Tech Coaching, or if you are interested in meeting other Tech Coaches, please visit www.AsktheTechCoach.com and check out our Free Resources, Blogs, and weekly Podcast.

Thank you for taking the time to read this.

Jeff Bradbury

ABOUT THE AUTHOR

Jeff Bradbury is a Technology Integration Specialist and Broadcast Journalism Teacher at West Rocks Middle School in Norwalk Connecticut and the creator of the TeacherCast Educational Network. With a background in Music Education, Jeff began performing in front of live audiences at a very early age and grew to love the opportunities he had working with others. This led him to earn his Bachelor of Science in Music Education in 2001 and eventually his Masters in Music Performance in Orchestral Conducting in 2010.

After several years of being a Music Director for both Orchestras and Opera Companies in the New York / Philadelphia region, including an opportunity to perform at Carnegie Hall he left the musical stage and began work on building the TeacherCast Educational Network.

Created as a passion project to assist teachers in understanding educational technology, Jeff recorded the first TeacherCast Podcast in the summer of 2011. Since then the TeacherCast Network has been accessed in almost 180 countries and has amassed a following of more than 50,000 followers on Social Media. With more than 1,000 audio and video podcasts recorded featuring more than 500 EdTech Companies and thousands of educators, TeacherCast is rated as one of the top 50 educational websites.

In 2018, Jeff created the TeacherCast Tech Coaches Network to support Instructional Technology Coaches and EducationalPodcasting.com, a learning portal to teach educators how to infuse podcasting into their curriculum.

Jeff Bradbury is a Google for EDU Certified Innovator & Trainer, Microsoft Innovative Educator Expert & Trainer, and a TEDx Speaker. In 2012, he was recognized as one of the Top 50 Educators Using Social Media at the inaugural Bammy Awards and was nominated three times in the category of Innovator of the Year.

Sought after as a professional development presenter, Jeff Bradbury, co-founder of Edcamp New Jersey, has presented at the ISTE & FETC and Podcast Movement Conferences, presented Keynote Addresses for Pearson, Podcast Mid-Atlantic Conference, and Columbia University's Teacher College.

Jeff is married to Jennifer and is the father of an amazing set of triplets.

SCHOOL LIBRARIANS: THE UNSUNG HEROES IN EDUCATION

Andrea Trudeau

A glimpse beyond the headlines and age-old stereotype to reveal the transformative power of school librarians of today.

One need not look far to find sobering headlines about cuts in library funding, the elimination of libraries and librarians, or even suggestions to replace libraries with Amazon or Google. In "The Calamity of the Disappearing School Libraries," the author notes, "From coast to coast, elementary and high school libraries are being neglected, defunded, repurposed, abandoned, and closed" (Kachel, 2015). Consequently, entire library collections are being removed from the shelves and redistributed to classrooms around schools while certified school librarians' jobs are eliminated altogether. It's no surprise that concerns are mounting among those in the profession; however, school librarians are being presented with an opportunity—a call to action. For decades, they have been pigeonholed into a stereotype of a matronly figure donning thick-rimmed glasses and a cardigan with her nose buried in a book, shushing all who enter the library. This couldn't be further from the truth. In the incredible modern digital age in which we all work and live, a school library is more vibrant than ever and a certified school librarian's role is more vital than ever.

Sketchnote by Dana Ladenburger

School librarians are community builders. They create a safe, comfortable, and welcoming environment that meet individuals' needs while bringing people together within the school community and creating valuable partnerships beyond the school walls.

School librarians are advocates. They ensure equity and accessibility for all, honoring students' identities and personal struggles through a carefully curated print and digital collection, which emphasize "mirrors, windows, and sliding glass doors" where students not only find themselves but may look outside of themselves and experience others' worlds (Bishop, 1990).

School librarians are trailblazers. They transform the library into a learning playground, where staff and students explore new concepts, teaching methods, or tools while provided with valuable individualized support and scaffolding along with guided reflection.

School librarians are innovators. They harness the power of instructional technology to redefine teaching and learning experiences while modeling and cultivating digital citizenship skills to help others navigate an oftentimes complex digital world.

School librarians are critical consumers. They model and lead the way in information literacy, curating resources for lessons and units and assisting students and staff in seeking out and attributing reliable, unbiased, current information and visual sources.

School librarians are storytellers. They capture the hearts and minds of students through their passion for literacy and through the exploration of various genres and formats, ultimately instilling a lifelong love of reading in others.

School librarians are makers. They develop incredible makerspaces with both low-tech and high-tech tools that encourage curiosity and wonder; provide opportunities for exploring, tinkering, and creating; and embrace failure while promoting a growth mindset.

School librarians are cheerleaders. They support students and staff tirelessly in the wide range of lessons, units, and activities throughout the school year while providing engaging and fun school-wide initiatives and events that emphasize creativity, community, and service learning.

School librarians are change agents. They evolve and adapt to remain educational leaders in a time when technology and education are progressing at an increasingly rapid pace.

School librarians are magic makers. They work in the heart of the school and their impact can be felt well beyond the library walls; they are interwoven into the fabric of the school culture and their influence is evident in the lessons, resources, and even in the mindset in classrooms all around the school.

Behind every reader, every green screen video, every APA citation, every virtual reality lesson, and every community outreach project is a certified school librarian. Certified school librarians are the often overlooked, unsung heroes in education who play a critical role in schools today.

We do not shush, and we will not be shushed.

REFERENCES

Bishop, R.S. (1990). Mirrors, windows and sliding glass doors. *Perspectives: Choosing and Using Books for the Classroom*, 6(3).

Kachel, D. (2015, July 13). The calamity of the disappearing school libraries. *The Conversation*. Retrieved July 26, 2019, from https://theconversation.com/the-calamity-of-the-disappearing-school-libraries-44498

Andrea Trudeau

ABOUT THE AUTHOR

Andrea Trudeau, M.S.Ed. (@Andrea_Trudeau) is a National Board Certified Teacher (EA/ELA), a Ph.D. student in Northern Illinois University's Instructional Technology program, and 22-year veteran in education with a variety of teaching roles at Alan B. Shepard Middle School in Deerfield District 109. Currently, she is a self-proclaimed "no-shh" librarian working in an active learning commons that breaks free of what is often thought of as the stereotypical library, embracing creativity, collaboration, risk-taking, and fun. Andrea is passionate about project-based learning, literacy, innovative digital tools and resources, as well as the Maker Movement. Most importantly, Andrea believes firmly that the learning commons is the heart of the school, and she works diligently to help all those in her school community feel welcome, valued, and connected.

TEACHERS DESERVE IT TOO

Amy Storer

Our teachers deserve to be in the conversation when it comes to professional learning.

PROFESSIONAL DEVELOPMENT

Before becoming an instructional coach, I didn't put a lot of thought into the why behind professional development. Sure, there were some that I attended that did not relate to my content area and/or some that I loved or didn't like all that much. But in my head, it was just something I had to do. Have you ever felt this way about professional development or maybe it just felt like something to "check off"?

It was during my second year as an instructional coach, that my views on my job role and professional development started to shift. This is similar to how I would adjust my teaching based on my students and their feedback. Actually, this happens quite a bit now that I'm an instructional coach. So much of what I valued and fostered in my classroom were the same things that I wanted for the teachers that I was blessed to work with.

Things like:

- the importance of building relationships and listening (really listening).
- voice and choice in how they wanted to learn.
- being a partner in the learning process.
- remembering that this is their journey, not mine.
- support, follow through, reflection, etc.

The list could go on and on.

I made it a goal to start looking for ways to transform professional development on my campus and in my district. I came across a book called *The Four O'Clock Faculty*, and a few of its core beliefs became the driving force behind my journey to "rogue PD." Designing and providing meaningful PD and honoring teacher voice, affects what students learn <u>and</u> how they learn it.

I had this sense of urgency to provide these experiences for my teachers. To give them what I worked so hard to give my students..."sticky learning"-Learning that sticks because it means something to them! Have I come across tons of road bumps on this journey? For sure. But the goal remains the same. I want my teachers to want to continue to grow in their field and content areas. I want professional learning to excite and inspire them.

A great place to start when beginning your journey to "rogue PD", is to survey your teachers. What are some things <u>they</u> would like to learn about? Use that input to design your professional learning calendar for the year.

Now, this next part was the part that I really enjoyed! The design process! I have always been fascinated with classroom teachers and administrators that transform the learning spaces for their students and teachers. Don't get me wrong. You don't have to jump on desks and dress up in costumes to impact your students or your teachers, but a huge shout-out to those that do this <u>for the impact on learning</u>!

I decided that I wanted to transform my space into something more than just a "PD Room." I wanted to set the tone by creating themes to engage my adult learners.

I offered things such as "Cookies with Your Coach," "Lemonade, Love and Lean on Me," "Tech or Treat," and "Appy Hour." Many of these ideas sparked from conversations that I had with other educators on Twitter and books such as *The Four O'Clock Faculty*. I would go to my local dollar store or Walmart and buy decorations and buy or make treats to match the theme. I am blessed to work on a campus where admin supports all of my crazy ideas and helps with funding them! (***Shout-out to one of the best principals I have ever worked for! Thank you for your love and support, Mallory Kirby!***)

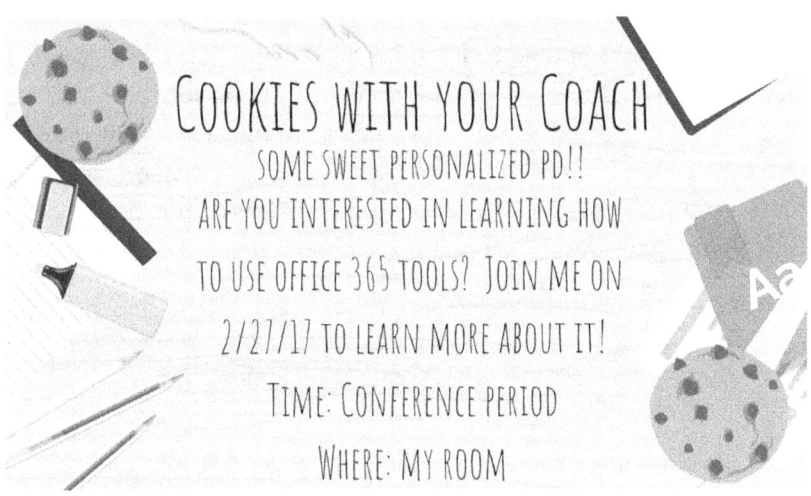

Image Created in Buncee

But just like in the classroom, you don't have to make these grand gestures to impact learning. The most important part of this journey for me was the learning. *This is why I always do my best to reframe professional development, by calling it professional learning.* I am now more mindful of the design of it, and the importance of designing in a way that reaches all types of learners. Decorating my room and providing snacks and setting the mood...that's the icing on the cake; the cherry on top.

Our teachers deserve to be a part of the conversation when it comes to professional learning. They deserve to have a seat at the table because this isn't about me or any other person that is in charge of teacher growth. It's their table, and it's about them! It is time to start honoring their voices in what they want to learn and how they want to learn it. Teachers deserve it too!

My goal for this school year? To make more professional learning available to my teachers by building a library of videos for them to access anywhere at anytime. One of my favorite creation tools to use as an instructional coach is Buncee. My goal is to create professional learning experiences by using this as well as a screencast tool. I will then save them to a curation site, such as Wakelet, so they can easily access it. Stay tuned!

I do want to leave you with this thought, though. Don't wait for your district or your campus to provide you with the professional learning that you want or need. I want to empower you to seek it out. Seek it out by joining a book study or hopping on a Twitter chat. Find teachers in your building or in your district to learn from. Spend some time listening to educational podcasts or books on tape.

As Rich Czyz, of the *Four O'Clock Faculty* says, "When no one else cares, you should."

Find a match to light the fire.

Keep learning and growing, my friends! You deserve it too!

Amy Storer

ABOUT THE AUTHOR

Amy Storer is an instructional coach and lead technology integration mentor in Montgomery, TX. She loves being an instructional coach and working alongside the wonderful educators of Keenan Elementary School. She is a distinguished educator that encourages and motivates others to reach far beyond the classroom walls to make learning more meaningful and inspiring. She has a true passion for working with other educators and students to empower them to make and foster global connections.

006# PART SIX: TELLING OUR STORIES

UNDRCAFF3INATED: A PODCAST STORY

Erin B. Kiger

A podcast story for real teachers who are real tired.

PD for real teachers

who are REAL tired
bit.ly/undrcaff3inatED_podcast

"LET'S DO A PODCAST!"

J oelle sent a message in our Voxer group. It didn't take very long for both Ashley and me to jump in with very excited versions of YES!

But now what? How do we start a podcast? Do we have anything to say that anyone wants to hear? How do we make it? What do we call it? When will we find the time? All of these questions were being thrown around in Voxer and at the same time we were mentally processing each answer, we were reassuring each other, and asking more questions. Through that night of what seemed like hours of Voxing, the only thing we knew was that we WERE starting a podcast together. The three of us, the dream team.

That was in September. Over the next couple of months, we worked on this idea. We really didn't know much about podcasting. Joelle had spoken with Matt Miller at ISTE 2018 about Anchor and she tried it with her class of fourth graders. I had heard of it from Scott Sheeler, a colleague at Ohio State, and tried it with him. Everyone said the same thing: it was easy, and we needed easy. The other thing we needed was short. Joelle shared that she loved Matt Miller's podcast because it was 15 minutes long. She could listen while she did the dishes, for example, but didn't feel like she would miss anything when she was done because the podcast was also over. She also liked that she could get in a good three or four episodes on a morning run. So, easy and short was where we started, but it wasn't easy or short to get started.

We continued to work through the details as we thought of them. Ashley created a Google Sheet and we brain dumped topic ideas. I created a whole Google account specifically for our podcast. Joelle knew how to create a logo, but before we could dive much further, we had to figure out what we were going to call ourselves.

In order to create social media accounts and our website, we needed to have a name—something that described us, peaked curiosity about our message, and something that listeners identified with. We started talking about being working moms, but what about dads? We tried coffee, but Joelle likes Diet Coke. We tried something about teacher parents, but we couldn't figure out anything.

During our conversations, we were all always so tired that we felt there was just never enough caffeine to keep up with everything between children, family, home, and work...and everything else. We finally we circled back to the coffee idea but shifted to caffeine, and the fact that we didn't ever have enough, and undercaffeinated came to life. After a little Twitter conversion, we finally arrived at undrcaff3inatED. The 3 comes from the fact that there are 3 of us and the missing first e comes from the fact that the name was too long for a Twitter handle.

Now we had the name, the accounts, the ideas, and clearly we had the excitement. We just had to get started with the next step...what is the next step? Well, after playing around in Anchor and listening to a couple of podcasts, we figured out we needed to have an introduction. I don't want to say we struggled with this, but we struggled with this. More specifically, we struggled with finding our collective voice for our intro. We worked on a Google Doc together to write a script; highlighting, crossing out, adding comments and suggestions, cutting and pasting, and starting over again completely, numerous times.

One night we all collectively worked from home on this doc, Voxing each other, when Joelle wrote something that included "PD for real teachers, who are real tired." That was it. That was what we needed. We had been trying to be too serious, too professional, too perfect. That's what was holding us up because while we are professional and hard-working, we are also very silly, and we wanted that humor and that joy to come across. We had to come to this realization again when we were recording our first few episodes 27 million times because they weren't perfect. And yes that number is exact (see, me being silly).

Looking back from that point, it's all a blur. We went from brainstorming to recording and I feel like I have no idea how. We were...we ARE publishing podcasts. And people are listening! Joelle and I went to ISTE 2019 this summer, in Philadelphia. With the help of another podcaster, Scott Nunes (who had been a guest on our show), I was handing out Undrcaff3inated stickers like crazy! As we were handing them out, I had teachers asking if it was my podcast, because they had heard it! AND LIKED IT!! I was so excited and still am. Teachers are listening; teachers are listening to Ashley, Joelle, and me! In my head is the clip of Sally Field saying "You like me!"

This is a passion project, there is no doubt. The 3 of us are doing this podcast because we want to continue to work together. The 3 of us are doing this podcast because we want to continue to learn: learn from other educators, learn about new tools and strategies, and learn how to support other educators. The three of us are doing this podcast because we want to have an impact on teachers, we want to ignite a fire, a passion, and inspire the excitement that we feel for the profession of education, regardless of your specific role.

And of course, while we podcast, you better believe Ashley and I will have our very large cups of coffee and Joelle will have her Diet Coke or two. Because we are doing this podcast to provide PD for real teachers who are real tired.

Erin B. Kiger

ABOUT THE AUTHOR

My name is Erin Kiger. I have worked in education for 15 years. I began working as a classroom teacher in 2004 and taught Kinder, 1st, 4th, 5th and technology for the first 8 years of my career. After earning my MEd in Curriculum and Instruction with a focus on Technology Integration, I left the classroom to support teachers with technology integration. Since 2012, I have supported teachers as both a technology and instructional coach. I have also been responsible for data collection and testing coordination.

In 2018, I earned an MA in Educational Leadership with a focus on Educational Technology. I decided to pursue a degree in Leadership for the same reason I decided to pursue my degree in Educational Technology. I was excited about the potential changes in education. I saw amazing educators sharing ideas that could revolutionize the way students learn. There were conversations happening that challenged me, inspired me, and gave me hope for the future of education. I wanted to be a part of those conversations, I wanted to share those conversations, and I wanted to encourage and inspire those conversations. Both degrees supported my dream of changing education.

On a more personal level, I have been married for 3 years to the man who is the calm to my storm as I juggle way too many endeavors. We have an amazing son who surprised us when he arrived 2 weeks early on the 4th of July. He brings so much joy, laughter, and light into our lives on a daily basis. I have an unhealthy obsession with Disney, I love old books because of the way they smell, and I will always pick the chocolate dessert. In the end, I'm always up for a new adventure, however that may look…a trip to the beach, a virtual tour of a dream vacation, a podcast with my colleagues Ashley and Joelle, a new job at a school on the opposite side of the country or writing a short snapshot for Edumatch!

I'm excited and honored to be able to share our podcast story with everyone.

FIRST IMPRESSIONS WILL MAKE A DIFFERENCE

Kristen Koppers, M.Ed., NBCT

When you finally see how others view you is not as accurate as your story should be and you change the way your narrative is told.

CREATING MY NARRATIVE

As a secondary education teacher of seventeen years and a National Board Certified Teacher (NBCT), I find myself searching how to tell my story. My story may seem similar to all other educators around the country -- but if you Googled my name, one of the first few sites that pop up is a "rate my teacher..." site. This site is barely used by students, but when it is, students are critical about the teacher, whether it's good or bad. Many students use this site to publicly denounce a teacher/professor on whether they like the person or not. It does not have anything to do with what is learned in the classroom. This is where someone else tells the story. What others see online is only a snapshot of an educator.

I first met Dr. Joe Sanfelippo, Superintendent of Fall Creek School District in Wisconsin, in 2015. He said it best, that no one will tell your story if you don't. At first it didn't matter to me what people say or don't say. But the more I listened to Joe, the more I understood what he meant. His keynote and workshops on "Changing the Narrative" focused on teachers telling their stories. "Promoting the positives helps shape the narrative and create a shared identity' (Sanfelippo and Sinais, 2017). The fact is that we need to brand ourselves in a way that connects back to ourselves so others will hear our stories. After that conference, I went back home and started to brand myself. I needed a way to tell my story through social media where my story could be heard among others.

So I thought why would I care what others say about me? But it wasn't about caring what was written on these sites, it was how my story was being written by others. Those online sites don't change who I am as a teacher. However the, "rate my sites" and comments written on social media change my story. I believe that others will believe what they want to hear or see; however, because it is my story, I have the ability to change it.

I can't write about growing up in a bad situation or having a bad childhood. I can't write a story about living with one parent or the other. And I can't write about my struggles to survive from rags to riches. But what I can write about is how I was able to overcome certain obstacles to being the educator I am today. This is the story that you won't find on social media or the "rate my…" sites.

My demeanor came from my father. He was a strong willed man who worked hard and cared deeply for his family. His ethics, determination and hard work is what was instilled in me at a very young age. But there was another side to my father that no one else saw -- his caring side. I inherited this from him too. My father did not let his feelings show to anyone, even me. It wasn't until he was dying from cancer that he and I secretly shared our feelings together until the day he passed. Neither one of us had to say anything to each other but we just knew. He only wanted the best for me where I was happy with who I am. While this may not be a struggle that I learned to overcome at the age of 6 months, it is still part of my story. I was born pigeon-toed where I had to wear casts on both of my legs to straighten my tendons out. I wore special shoes to ensure my legs and feet were straight. Another part of my story is losing my grandfather when I was sixteen years old and not even knowing my other grandfather. Part of my struggle was to fit in through school and not be excluded all the time, and part of my struggle was to have a child after being told that it would never happen. Going from doctor to doctor, medical treatment after medical treatment to giving birth to a son eleven years after I was married. This is part of my story that many do not know. But yet, they seem to post about who I am as a person and a teacher.

THE REASON I LEARNED HOW TO CHANGE MY NARRATIVE

Like any child, I used to play school and be the teacher. I wanted to assign work and grade papers. But playing school was not the same as being a teacher. Throughout my childhood, I learned to be strong because we all know how kids can be to other kids (and I was that other kid). But the strength my father instilled in me continued to help me pursue my writing career. Rejection after rejection came from magazines, newspapers, and publishers. Now with most people, some stories stop there... but not mine. During high school, I continued writing for the TV network and school newspaper where this continued throughout college. Despite the fact that my high school journalism teacher told me to quit writing because I would never make it as a journalist, it pushed me harder to prove him wrong. Four years after graduating high school, I graduated with a Bachelor of Arts degree in Journalism / English with a practical writing minor.

At this point, I want to state that it was not the teacher who pushed me to prove him wrong. I want to include how there are teachers that truly care about students and those who earn a paycheck. It was not because of him that I graduated to earn a Bachelor's degree, but it was from my parents that I learned to not listen to what others tell me as they did not know me. As Dr. Sanfelippo asked the audience of educators, "when was the last time something amazing happened in your school?" I really connected to his question because in my class, my students do amazing stuff all the time. Yet, no one knows about it. I can understand the feelings my students have when they are not acknowledged for their amazing accomplishments. So I created my brand by creating a hashtag on Twitter to share the stories of my students and their successes. I wanted to learn how to connect with my students unlike my teachers who were not able to connect with me.

FOCUS ON STUDENT ACHIEVEMENT

There are several different types of teachers that students encounter throughout their education. Each teacher has his/her own story. As stated previously, my story may seem similar to other teachers. However, my teaching became a story within itself.

Students who are in my class understand the knowledge they will gain. They know when they walk through the door to expect the unexpected. I will challenge them to be the best that they can, but will work with them to ensure understanding and comprehension. They will learn to use their critical thinking skills while focusing on soft skills needed prior to graduation. They are not discredited or stopped from voicing their own opinion. I believe that each student has his/her own story and behind that story has knowledge. I can't deny my students the opportunity to share their thoughts in an English classroom as interpretation and analysis is the key to understanding. From this, they will learn and grow from each other, especially through collaboration.

DON'T LET OTHERS TELL YOUR STORY FOR YOU

What the negative comments and ratings found on social media and the "rate my..." sites state are inaccurate as they are personal feelings from students that may not be happy with their grade. While some may think I am a hard grader or unwilling to help, those become personal feelings that ultimately tell my story without accuracy. While I cannot change how these past students feel, I can change how my future students tell the story of their learning. Teaching is not an easy profession for anyone because many are telling your story. I learned that if I do not tell my story someone else will in their own way.

I do understand that the desire to learn does not come easily with teenagers. For me, each school year and each class hour there is a new class of 28-30 students. Just like they do not know my story, I do not know theirs. By knowing and understanding my students, it helps me to grow as a person as well as instilling the desire for them to learn. As part of my belief in teaching, I encourage my past, present, and future students to succeed in everything they do as I push them to be better than they were yesterday and how they can be better than tomorrow. Ultimately, I encourage my students to try their best. The word "encouragement" can have multiple meanings; however, if the right definition is not utilized properly, the word becomes useless. Students learn, quickly, that the word encouragement does not necessarily apply just in teaching. In fact, many of my students have learned that the word helps them in sports and other activities. I don't want anyone else to tell their story like mine has been told throughout the years. I wanted them to use their education as a foundation, a stepping stone, to write their own story and by using their knowledge, students are able to see the value of their education. Because we never stop learning, teaching is a continuous cycle of where we've been and where we are headed. As a teacher, it's my passion to explain how education is invaluable. We all have a story, and instead of allowing others to tell it based on second-hand information, misperceptions, or a self-imposed autobiographical layer, we need to devote time to this important aspect of our professions" (Sanfelippo and Sinansis, 2017).

Students know my name even before walking into my classroom. They walk in with mixed feelings of what to expect. They listened in the halls, they read comments on social media, and, perhaps, they even read the ratings on online sites. We learn that the first impression leaves a big impact on others. And first impressions can only be made once. But what if that first impression is not by me? This is a common concern among many people as others can diminish one's credibility even before the first impression.

After almost three decades of submitting my writings and being rejected, I was given a chance to share my knowledge. I share this information with my students because I want to share my story of certain struggles that I had to go through just as they have their own struggles to overcome. I don't want their story to be told by others; I want them to tell their own story in their own words.

REFERENCE

Sanfelippo, J., & Sinansis, T. (2017, September/October). Telling Your Story. Retrieved July 18, 2019, from https://www.naesp.org/sites/default/files/SanfelippoSinanis_SO17.pdf

Kristen Koppers, M.Ed., NBCT

ABOUT THE AUTHOR

Kristen Koppers, M.Ed., NBCT, is a blogger, presenter, self-published author, and high school educator as well as an adjunct professor at a local junior college. She has been teaching for more than fifteen years and is currently teaching high school English in Illinois. She is a Google Certified Educator and National Board Certified Teacher. Kristen has a Master's degree in English and a second Master's degree in Education Administration. Kristen wrote the book *Differentiated*

Instruction in the Teacher Profession as a way to share her ideas of how to use Differentiated Instruction inside the classroom. As an educator, it is important to find innovative ways to meet the needs of students. Kristen is often on Twitter (@Mrs_Koppers) participating in chats and collaborating with other educators. It's easy to share DI ideas on Twitter (#DITeaching). Website: (https://kristenkoppers.wixsite.com/koppers)

NOTES

6. GOING GRADELESS

1. https://twitter.com/markbarnes19?lang=en
2. https://www.edweek.org/ew/articles/2018/01/10/no-students-dont-need-grades.html
3. https://www.alfiekohn.org/
4. https://teachersgoinggradeless.com/
5. https://twitter.com/tg2chat?lang=en

11. GAMING BUSINESS EDUCATION - LET'S PLAY!

1. http://gamesineducation.org/symposium/
2. http://www.cdc.gov/ncbddd/autism/data.html

15. PREPARING FOR THE FUTURE

1. https://www.globenewswire.com/news-release/2016/10/06/992265/0/en/New-Study-Finds-Freelance-Economy-Grew-to-55-Million-Americans-This-Year-35-of-Total-U-S-Workforce.html

OTHER EDUMATCH TITLES

EduMatch Snapshot in Education (2016)
In this collaborative project, twenty educators located throughout the United States share educational strategies that have worked well for them, both with students and in their professional practice.

The #EduMatch Teacher's Recipe Guide
Editors: Tammy Neil & Sarah Thomas
Dive in as fourteen international educators share their recipes for success, both literally and metaphorically!

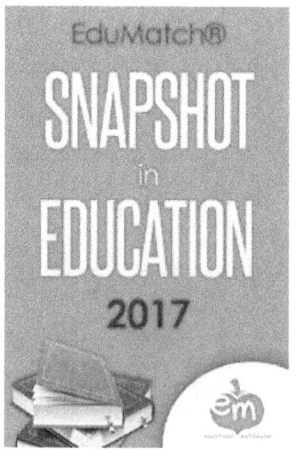

EduMatch Snapshot in Education (2017)
We're back! EduMatch proudly presents Snapshot in Education (2017). In this two-volume collection, 32 educators and one student share their tips for the classroom and professional practice.

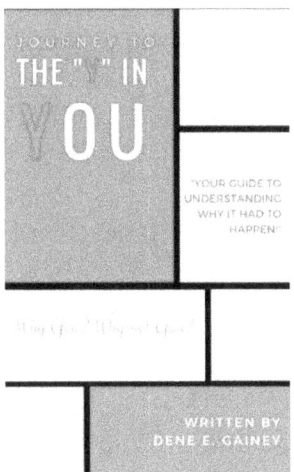

Journey to The "Y" in You by Dene Gainey
This book started as a series of separate writing pieces that were eventually woven together to form a fabric called The Y in You. The question is, "What's the 'why' in you?"

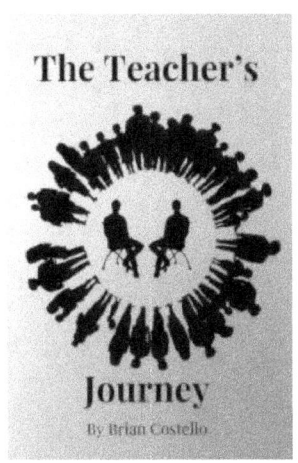

The Teacher's Journey by Brian Costello
Follow the Teacher's Journey with Brian as he weaves together the stories of seven incredible educators. Each step encourages educators at any level to reflect, grow, and connect.

The Fire Within
Compiled and edited by Mandy Froehlich
Adversity itself is not what defines us. It is how we react to that adversity and the choices we make that creates who we are and how we will persevere.

EduMagic by Sam Fecich
This book challenges the thought that "teaching" begins only after certification and college graduation. Instead, it describes how students in teacher preparation programs have value to offer their future colleagues, even as they are learning to be teachers!

Makers in Schools
Editors: Susan Brown & Barbara Liedahl
The maker mindset sets the stage for the Fourth Industrial Revolution, empowering educators to guide their students.

Divergent EDU by Mandy Froehlich
The concept of being innovative can be made to sound so simple. But what if the development of the innovative thinking isn't the only roadblock?

EduMatch Snapshot in Education (2018)
EduMatch® is back for our third annual Snapshot in Education. Dive in as 21 educators share a snapshot of what they learned, what they did, and how they grew in 2018.

Daddy's Favorites by Elissa Joy
Illustrated by Dionne Victoria

Five-year-old Jill wants to be the center of everyone's world. But, her most favorite person in the world, without fail, is her Daddy. But Daddy has to be Daddy, and most times that means he has to be there when everyone needs him, especially when her brother Danny needs him.

Level Up Leadership by Brian Kulak
Gaming has captivated its players for generations and cemented itself as a fundamental part of our culture. In order to reach the end of the game, they all need to level up.

DigCit Kids edited by Marialice Curran & Curran Dee
This book is a compilation of stories, starting with our own mother and son story, and shares examples from both parents and educators on how they embed digital citizenship at home and in the classroom.

Stories of EduInfluence by Brent Coley
In Stories of EduInfluence, veteran educator Brent Coley shares stories from more than two decades in the classroom and front office.

The Edupreneur by Dr. Will
The Edupreneur is a 2019 documentary film that takes you on a journey into the successes and challenges of some of the most recognized names in K-12 education consulting.

OTHER EDUMATCH TITLES

In Other Words by Rachelle Dene Poth
In Other Words is a book full of inspirational and thought-provoking quotes that have pushed the author's thinking and inspired her.

To Whom it May Concern
Editors: Sarah-Jane Thomas, PhD & Nicol R. Howard, PhD
In *To Whom it May Concern...*, you will read a collaboration between two Master's in Education classes at two universities on opposite coasts of the United States.

One Drop of Kindness by Jeff Kubiak
This children's book, along with each of you, will change our world as we know it. It only takes *One Drop of Kindness to fill a heart with love.*

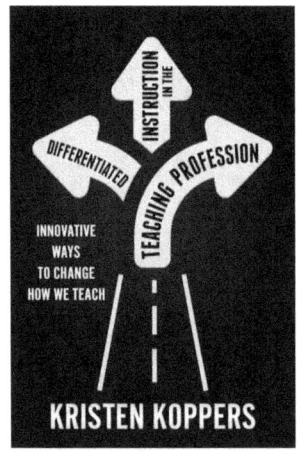

Differentiated Instruction in the Teaching Profession by Kristen Koppers
Differentiated Instruction in the Teaching Profession is an innovative way to use critical thinking skills to create strategies to help all students succeed. This book is for educators of all levels who want to take the next step into differentiating their instruction.

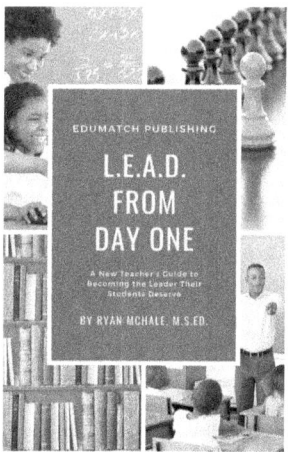

L.E.A.D. from Day One by Ryan McHale
L.E.A.D. from Day One is a go-to resource to help educators outline a future plan toward becoming a teacher leader. The purpose of this book is to help you see just how easily you can transform your entire mindset to become the leader your students need you to be.

Unlock Creativity by Jacie Maslyk
Every classroom is filled with creative potential. *Unlock Creativity* will help you discover opportunities that will make every student see themselves as a creative thinker.

Make Waves! by Hal Roberts

In *Make Waves!* Hal discusses 15 attributes of a great leader. He shares his varied experience as a teacher, leader, a player in the N.F.L., and a plethora of research to take you on a journey to emerge as leader of significance.

21 Lessons of Tech Integration Coaching by Martine Brown

In *21 Lessons of Tech Integration Coaching*, Martine Brown provides a practical guide about how to use your skills to support and transform schools.

Everyone Can Learn Math by Alice Aspinall
How do you approach a math problem that challenges you? Do you keep trying until you reach a solution? Or are you like Amy, who gets frustrated easily and gives up?

EduMagic Shine On by Sam Fecich, Katy Gibson, Hannah Sansom, and Hannah Turk
EduMagic: A Guide for New Teachers picks up where *EduMagic: A Guide for Preservice Teachers* leaves off. Dr. Sam Fecich is back at the coffee shop and is now joined by three former students-turned-friends. She is excited to introduce you to these three young teachers: Katy Gibson, Hannah Sansom, and Hannah Turk.

All In by Kristen Nan & Jacie Maslyk

Unlike Nevada's slogan of "what happens in Vegas, stays in Vegas," this book reminds us that what happens in the classroom, should never stay within the classroom! It spotlights a unique relationship between a forward-thinking teacher and a future-focused district administrator.

www.ingramcontent.com/pod-product-compliance
Lightning Source LLC
Chambersburg PA
CBHW071233070526
44583CB00017B/2159